"yikes! it's due tomorrow?!"
How to Handle SCHOOL SNAFUS

a *Go Parents!* guide™

Carmella Van Vleet

Nomad Press

A division of Nomad Communications

10 9 8 7 6 5 4 3 2 1

Copyright © 2004 Carmella Van Vleet

The trademark "Nomad Press" and the Nomad Press logo are trademarks of
Nomad Communications, Inc. "a Go Parents! guide™" is a trademark of
Nomad Communications, Inc. Printed in the United States.

ISBN 0-9722026-8-4

Questions regarding the ordering of this book should be addressed to
The Independent Publishers Group
814 N. Franklin St.
Chicago, IL 60610
www.ipgbook.com

Nomad Press, 2456 Christian Street, White River Junction, VT 05001
www.nomadpress.net

Contents

Dedication

This one is for Jim because with him by my side,
I can handle anything.

Acknowledgments

At the risk of sounding like someone who wins an Oscar and then thanks everyone she's ever met in her acceptance speech, I'd like to acknowledge some people who made this book possible.

First of all, I'd like to thank my editor, Lauri Berkenkamp, for believing in me and my idea, and for writing such great parenting guides. Coming into an existing series is like being a substitute teacher; I'm honored you trusted me to take over your classroom for a while.

Second, many thanks to all those teachers, parents, and other experts who told me when I got it right or wrong: Jeremy Arend, Carol Condon, Barbara Kanninen, Carolyn Markowsky, Christine Naylor, Kim Newlon, Marian Van Vleet. And to Leslie Davison, whose school snafu inspired this book—how's this for a silver lining?

To my friends who shared advice and ideas and didn't complain when I called to say, "Listen to this paragraph and tell me what you think." Beth Comer, Tess Ellis, Kim Juttner, and Jen Richards— a big thank you.

I'd also like to thank my family, the one scattered about the country and especially the one I live with: Jim, Matt, Sam, and Abbey. Without you, there is no me. (Sorry for all the times I forgot to start dinner because I was writing!)

And finally, I have an armful of gratitude for my father, Darrell W. Condon. Dad, you are the only reason I was able to finish this book. Thank you for being my bridge over troubled water.

—C.V.V.

Nobody Said There'd Be a Test!

Ah . . . fall. That time of year when parents finally get to hear the three little words they've been longing for: back to school.

But sending your child off to school can really test your patience and imagination. For example, what do you do if your child is afraid to use the bathroom at school? Or if your daughter is convinced her teacher is out to get her? How about when your son waits until bedtime to tell you he has a big project due the next day? And, for Pete's sake, what do you do with all that art that comes home?!

Don't panic—help is at hand. *How to Handle School Snafus* is a humorous and practical guide to handling common grade-school problems. Whether your child is afraid of the school's automatic flushing toilets, nervous about having a male teacher for the first time, or is suffering from test anxiety or a nasty case of spring fever, *How to Handle School Snafus* has the answers. Just think of it as Cliff Notes for those "parenting pop quizzes" kids like to give.

How to Use This Book

This book should be used as a guide; when it comes to handling a school snafu, there is no one right answer. The snafus listed in this book are some common problems and exasperating I-haven't-the-foggiest-idea-what-to-do-about-that-one roadblocks many families will encounter during the grade-school years. The kid-tested suggestions come from parents, teachers, and other experts and combine good, old-fashioned common sense with a dose of humor. Let's face it, with some school-related challenges—like when you don't know how to do your first grader's homework—all you can do is cry, bribe someone, or have a good laugh.

How to Handle School Snafus can be read straight through or used to look up a particular situation as needed. Each chapter begins with a brief introduction and then addresses a variety of snafus, including numerous sidebars, insider tips, and interesting facts.

Are you getting ready for the new school year? Read **Chapter One: School's Back in Session!** for some ideas to start the year off right. Is your child dawdling in the mornings or having problems on the bus? Try **Chapter Two: "Hurry Up. You'll Be Late!"** **Chapter Three: Teacher From the Black Lagoon** offers advice on handling all those snafus that come up during the school day, including personality clashes with teachers, acting up in class, and lunchroom problems. It's time to hit the books in **Chapter Four: Making the Grade**, where challenges such as test anxiety, cheating, and dealing with underachievers are addressed.

Is your child having trouble with friends? **Chapter Five: It's a Jungle Gym Out There** is devoted to problems with friends, bullies, teasing, and peer pressure. If homework hassles are making your head ache, take a peek in **Chapter Six: "Mom, My Project Is Due Tomorrow!"** for some ideas on creating healthy homework habits as well as some solutions for dealing with your young perfectionist or procrastinator. And finally, if you're up for a little boost in your grade as a parent, read **Chapter Seven: Extra Credit** for creative solutions to a few other snafus such as an avalanche of art, spring fever, volunteering at school, and teacher gift ideas.

Not to worry. For many parents, the first day of school is the beginning of not only their child's education but their own education in handling school snafus, as well.

And you thought your days of lessons, tests, and homework were over.

Chapter 1

School's Back In:
Handling Snafus Before The First Bell

You've endured shopping trips for the latest fashions with your picky son, taken out a small loan to buy him shoes, picked through hundreds of lunchboxes for just the right one, gone on a scavenger hunt for school supplies, and filled out so many forms that you can recite the pediatrician's address by heart.

Getting your child ready for school may be a test of your shopping (and budgeting) skills, but it's only half the battle. There are so many new things to experience that sending your child off to school can be a test of courage—yours and your child's.

Unfortunately, the Parent Handbook the school sent home doesn't really have the answers. (It does, however, say your son's new shoes won't be allowed because they have dark soles that could scuff the gym floor.)

"I've Got Who?!"

It's the week before school starts and there's a crowd by the front doors of the school. Everyone is chatting nervously. Finally, what everyone has been waiting for is posted: the class lists.

Your son scans the lists. "Oh, man! I've got Mrs. Walters!" he says, obviously unhappy.

While moving up a grade or starting school for the first time is exciting, a new teacher can also be a little frightening. Parents and kids alike hear stories about the teachers in their school and sometimes a teacher's reputation can precede her or him. Students and parents may even have previous experience with a teacher that causes anxiety when class lists are posted. Or, sometimes, it's a specific characteristic causing your child to worry.

As a general rule, once class lists are posted, they are set in stone. Most schools, afraid of setting precedents, will not make changes. This is why lists are frequently posted a day or two before class starts. The theory is parents are less likely to argue a placement if there's not much time to pursue the issue. That is not to say all is lost if you or your child are unhappy about whose class he or she will be in. Here are a few tips to ease the anxiety:

Give the teacher a chance. If you're feeling uneasy, meet the teacher and talk to her. See what she's like. Ask about her approach with the kids or why she went into teaching. Put aside any preconceived notions you have and appreciate the teacher for who she is and the gifts she can bring to your child.

Talk to other parents or students who have had the teacher. You may have heard horror stories from some people but remember, you're probably not getting the whole story. Ask other students and parents about their experiences. Chances are you'll hear things like: "He gives a lot of homework but his space unit is a ton of fun!" or "He's tough but the kids really seemed to love him."

Give your child time to adjust. Getting used to a new teacher and her classroom style can take some time. Encourage your child to give her teacher a few weeks and to keep an open mind. Often times, the teacher your child hates at the beginning of the year is the same teacher she tearfully hugs good-bye in June!

Meeting the Teacher for the First Time

If you're meeting your child's teacher for the first time at an Open House, it's best to keep things fairly brief. After you've introduced yourself, introduce your child. (You can also encourage your child to introduce herself.) Make sure you let the teacher know if your child has a nickname she prefers to go by. Save any long

HAVING A MALE TEACHER FOR THE FIRST TIME

Male teachers are a rare sight in many elementary school districts. This is too bad—men can have a wonderful impact on young students, connecting with kids and bringing experiences to them in unique ways. For example, it's great having a male teacher around when it comes time for older students to divide up for sex education in health class. Male teachers can also be great role models for children who don't have a positive male figure in their lives.

Because male teachers at the elementary level are such a novelty, plenty of children—and parents—have a hard time adjusting. There are many myths about male teachers: they're tougher than women, they're mean, they're less affectionate, they're not as creative. But, like their female counterparts, male teachers come in a variety of sizes, shapes, and personalities. Fortunately, many children and parents quickly adjust and their worries can be put to rest.

conversations or concerns for another time when the teacher isn't trying to meet and greet thirty other sets of parents and kids. Before saying good-bye, be sure to let the teacher know you and your child are looking forward to a great year.

When Friends Are in Different Classes

You're standing by, chatting with other parents, as your daughter checks the class list. All of a sudden, she comes running over. "There must be a mistake!" she says. "My best friend and I aren't in the same class! How can I go to school without her? The whole, entire year is ruined!"

Though you suspect the whole year isn't ruined, it's clear the first few days of school are going to be rough. Being separated from friends can be quite upsetting. This is especially true for girls, who tend to have close attachments to one or two friends whereas boys tend to run with a larger group of friends and have looser ties.

Because you can't change things, all you can do is help your child accept the situation

INSIDER TIP

Touching base with the teacher before the school year is especially important if you have a child with special needs, regardless if those needs have been addressed in an I.E.P. Consider meeting the teacher without your child present at first. This will give a teacher who has little or no experience with your child's needs to ask questions. It will also give you a chance to give the teacher information that your child might be uncomfortable sharing.

and make the best of it. (It probably won't make your child feel any better, but you might find solace in knowing that often times splitting up friends turns out to be a good thing in the long run. It gives children a chance to interact with different people and can cut down on the socializing that sometimes interferes with learning.) Here's how you can help your child deal with being in a different class than her friend:

Let your child express her disappointment. Validate the friendship and your child's feelings by saying something like, "It's hard to be apart from our friends, isn't it?"

Arrange for her to spend time with the friend. Let your child know that you will do whatever you can to support her spending time with her friend. Remind her that she can still see her friend at recess, lunch, on the bus, and after school.

Encourage your child to seek out new friends in her classroom or cultivate other friendships. Share the old saying, "Make new friends but keep the old. One is silver and the other gold."

Help her realize her goal should be to add a friend or two, not replace the other friend. Do this by telling her things like, "You and so-and-so always had a great time. You'll always be friends, but it's okay to have fun and be friends with other kids, too."

It's Tough Being the New Kid

As Kermit the Frog told us, "It's not easy being green." And as any kid who's moved or changed schools can tell you, "It's not easy being new."

Moving can bring a mix of emotions and challenges to children. They may be excited or nervous or, quite often, both! When it comes to moving to a new school, children ages five to twelve are most concerned with how their routines will change. Knowing this can make your job as a parent a bit easier. If your child is taking his turn at being "the new kid at school" there are a few things you can do to make the transition go more smoothly.

First, take your child to visit his or her new school before the first day. If you're making the change in the fall, visit the school a week before it opens. (Teachers and other school staff are usually around, preparing for the year.) If you're coming in mid-year, visit a week or so before your child's first day. Calling ahead of time is a good idea so you don't show up on an atypical day such as Career Day or a Proficiency Test day. When you call, ask if there's another student, preferably in your child's class or grade, who

INSIDER TIP

Being new is stressful. Adjusting can take a lot of time and energy—time and energy that used to be devoted to schoolwork! Occasionally, a child's grades may temporarily slip. Grades may also suffer as your child either tries to catch up with his class or get into sync with them if he's ahead. Try not to worry about these slips and respect that your child's most important job, for the time being, is finding his place in the new school.

can show you and your child around. When you arrive, let your child check out the layout of the building. Help him or her find all the important areas or rooms—his or her classroom, locker, the bathrooms, water fountains, office, library, gym, art room, computer lab, cafeteria, playground, and bus drop-off area.

Second, be sure to ask about routines and rules. This is where another student would be most helpful. How does the lunchroom work, or is there a special "quiet" signal the teachers in the building use? Ask if there's a rule about needing hall passes (or, if you're a parent, a visitor's pass). Do students have IDs? Do they have to wear special shoes for gym? Are students required to work silently in the mornings or are they allowed to visit quietly in their classrooms before the bell rings? Try to get as much detail as you can about your child's day. The more your child knows about what's expected, the more comfortable he or she will be.

Finally, during the first few weeks of school, encourage your child to smile, talk, ask questions, and join in. Let him know that by opening up and being friendly and participating in activities, he will come across as approachable.

You should also encourage your child to be himself; don't agree to a drastic new hairstyle or wild wardrobe change or anything that will attract attention. Encourage your child to get the "lay of the land" first.

Fear of Getting Lost at School

Even a child who is not new to a school building may worry about getting lost. After all, your child will likely be in a new room or even in a new hall or section of the building. There are a few things you can do to ease a worried mind.

One. Take advantage of any Open House the school offers. Help your son find his classroom and see who his teacher and classmates are. Encourage him to find his desk or table and then explore the room. Afterward walk your child around the entire school. Point out any landmarks he can use to find his classroom. ("My room is by the office.") You might even discover the school itself has made efforts to help students by putting up signs, arrows, or colored tiles in hallways.

Two. Help your child draw a map. Creating a map of the school not only gives children a sense of control over their fears but provides a reference they can use when they get disoriented.

Three. Ask if there will be parent volunteers helping to direct new students the first few days of school. If there isn't one already, organize a welcoming committee!

Four. Use a variety of games to help your child get oriented to the school building.

Grades K through 2

Bingo. Make visiting school fun by putting together Bingo cards with squares for things like cafeteria, flag, office, water fountain, kid-sized chair, your child's room number, teacher, chalk, and so forth. Give your child a marker or stickers to cover each square as the two of you come across each item. Make several cards and play along with your child or let siblings (or friends) join in.

How Many Steps? After locating your child's classroom, help your child count off how many steps it takes to get to other places in the building. For example, "It takes one-hundred steps to get to the office." Or "It takes fifteen steps to get to the bathroom." Not only will your younger child get great counting practice, but he or she will also begin to get a sense of distance. ("The office is far away. The bathroom is close.")

"School" Book. Many teachers, especially those in the younger grades, have students put together class books about their tours around school. Help your child put together his or her own book by bringing along a camera and snapping

pictures when you visit. Once you're home, put the pictures in order. (What do you see first when you walk in the school building?) Add a description such as "The gym. Location: Right across from my classroom." You can also include pictures of school staff in the book so your child can learn the names and faces of those he or she will see each day.

Grades 3 through 6

Scavenger Hunt. Before you and your child visit school, prepare a list of things for your child to find and check off. Older kids love scavenger hunts and will benefit from a review of the building. Make the scavenger hunt even more challenging by writing riddles. For example, "This is the place where you'd find / teachers who are the hushing kind." (The library.)

Where in the School is Stu Dent? This activity is a fun variation of the game *Where in the World is Carmen San Diego?* Either you or your child describe various rooms or places in the school and see if the other one can figure out where Stu Dent is hiding. If you have a map of the school (or have made your own), add to the game by having your child use his fingers to "walk" around the school and search for Stu.

Imagination Maze. This game will test your child's sense of direction and knowledge of the school layout—and yours. Have your child close her eyes and take her on an imaginary "trip" out of her classroom and to another part of the school building. Use details such as, "You're passing the library now. The room you're looking for is on the right." Once your child finds the room or figures out where you've taken her, switch roles.

Separation Anxiety

Kindergartners

You fed your daughter a healthy breakfast. You helped her pack her freshly labeled supplies in her new backpack. You drove her to school, walked her to her classroom and stayed for a few minutes until she found a puzzle to work on. And, now, the big moment has arrived. It's time for you to leave.

"Ah, freedom," you sigh as you wave to your angel and turn to go.

Moments later, your daughter tackles you in the hall, throws her arms around your legs and wails so loudly several people poke their heads out of the classrooms to see who's being tortured. The teacher comes out to help you peel your daughter off. "I was so close I could taste it," you say.

If your little one is carrying on as if it's the end of the world, remember this: almost all children who are upset as they climb onto the bus or go into their classrooms quickly settle down and enjoy the day. Don't sit around fretting about your child being miserable. Trust the teacher—if your son or daughter continued to be inconsolable you would have been called.

Even kids who run into someplace new without so much as a backward glance at Mom and Dad can find going to school for the first time overwhelming. Does this mean you're destined to live life as a tackle dummy? Nope.

Separation anxiety is typically caused by children's fears for their parents. Much in the same way parents worry about their children's safety, children are concerned about their parents' welfare! They feel the need to protect Mom and Dad and so they start making up excuses or complaints about going to school. Reassuring your child that you'll be just fine without him or her may help the situation. In addition to this: Keep your own emotions on an even keel. Don't get all teary-eyed when you talk to your child about starting school. Your child might misinterpret these signs to mean school is a bad place to go. Also, tell your child what you're going to do or where you're going to be during the day. This may help put her mind at ease about your safety and help her picture you in her mind when she gets lonesome or anxious. On the flip side, don't go on and on about all your wonderful plans for your kid-free day. Going to the store and then out to lunch may sound a whole lot better than going to school to your child, and she may cling believing she can talk you into taking her too!

Separation anxiety may be heightened by the fear of the unknown, so let your child know ahead of time what to expect. For example, give her a heads-up about how many kids are in her class. (There might have been only a handful in the room during orientation.) Also, let your child know how long school will be. Since kids frequently have trouble with the concept of time, compare the time to something she knows. For example, "School will last as long as it takes to watch your favorite movie." Or give your child a time landmark such as: "I'll pick you up after your second recess." If possible, find out if a friend or neighbor will be in her class so she can seek out the familiar face. (All kids, rookies and veterans of the playground, will feel better if they know one or two classmates.) If you can't find out the class schedule ahead of time, a general overview such as "You'll probably read a book, have lunch, and play on the playground," might do the trick.

Don't give in to your bus-riding child's pleas for you to drop her off or pick her up from school. This goes for agreeing to eat lunch with your child everyday, as well. There's nothing wrong with doing these things, of course, but waiting until your anxious child has settled into a routine is best. Not only does giving in tell your child she's in control, not you, but it says you don't believe she can handle school on her own.

A little anxiety is normal during the first few weeks of school. If your child continues to have a hard time being away from you, talk to your child's teacher. Ask if there's a particular time of the day that is hard for your child. (Many kids are fine until after lunch or the afternoon when they get tired.) Brainstorm together. Maybe your child can carry a picture of the two of you together or another small token to take out when she's sad or can be allowed to write a note, draw a picture, or visit an older sibling when she's lonesome for Mom and Dad.

Older Students

Kindergartners don't have the market cornered on separation anxiety. Plenty of older kids have a hard time saying good-bye to Mom and Dad in the mornings, too. Some kids just don't like transitions or changes of any kind or, like "first-timers" or new kids, many of these children are simply anxious about the unknown. Because older children are less likely to come right out and tell you that they don't want to be away from you, or because they may not know what is causing their distress, an older child with separation anxiety will often act out. For example, they may dawdle in the mornings. They may also "suddenly" remember something very important they need to talk about, misplace shoes or homework, or complain about aches and pains on the way out the door or on the drive to school. Then again, they might come right out and say, "I don't want to go to school because I miss you!"

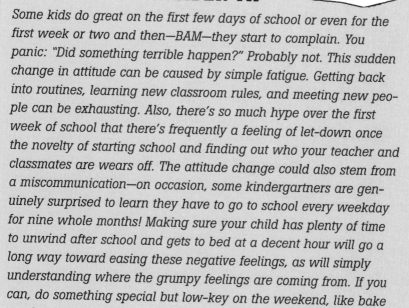

INSIDER TIP

Some kids do great on the first few days of school or even for the first week or two and then—BAM—they start to complain. You panic: "Did something terrible happen?" Probably not. This sudden change in attitude can be caused by simple fatigue. Getting back into routines, learning new classroom rules, and meeting new people can be exhausting. Also, there's so much hype over the first week of school that there's frequently a feeling of let-down once the novelty of starting school and finding out who your teacher and classmates are wears off. The attitude change could also stem from a miscommunication—on occasion, some kindergartners are genuinely surprised to learn they have to go to school every weekday for nine whole months! Making sure your child has plenty of time to unwind after school and gets to bed at a decent hour will go a long way toward easing these negative feelings, as will simply understanding where the grumpy feelings are coming from. If you can, do something special but low-key on the weekend, like bake a cake or rent a video, to celebrate a great start to the school year.

There are several things parents can do to ease their older children's anxiety:

Give your child a heads-up about his or her new routine. Find out about what your child can expect each day. What is the morning routine? What days does your child's class have gym, music, art, library, or go to the computer lab? How many recesses will your child have? Having as many details as possible will help your anxious child feel more in control.

Provide your child with a security item to hold onto or look at when he or she is nervous. It doesn't have to be expensive: a piece of costume jewelry, an old penny, a small rock, or even a piece of string to "remind" them of home! Wearing a watch comforts many older kids; they use it to keep track of how long they have until they go home. It gives them a sense of control and lets them anticipate the day.

Write notes to your child and hide them in his or her lunch box or backpack. You're never too old to enjoy finding a note from your mom or dad in an unexpected place.

Come up with a secret signal. Some kids' anxiety is at its highest just as the day is beginning. To help your child get off to a positive start (and keep all the embarrassing mushy stuff to a minimum), the two of you can use a secret signal that means, "I love you."

Don't forget to talk to your child's teacher. He may have some insight into why your child is hesitant to come to school or offer some other suggestions to try. At the very least, you might be comforted to discover that the same child who clings to your car door handle every morning and wails about not wanting to go into school is perfectly happy once you're out of the school driveway.

Chapter 2

"Hurry Up, You'll Be Late!": The Trouble Getting There

A thunderstorm knocked out the power in the middle of the night so the alarm didn't go off. There's no milk in the fridge. And the kids—who aren't even dressed yet, thank you very much—are fighting over who gets the prize from the cereal box. There are homework pages and projects scattered all over the place and you've already started writing the "Please excuse Jack and Susie for being late" note for school.

It's definitely one of those mornings when you wish you could just go back to bed and stay there.

Sometimes half the fun . . . er . . . battle is just getting there!

Getting Out the Door

Dawdling in the Mornings

It took your daughter twenty minutes to pick out what she wanted to wear. (And then she changed her mind.) Now she's eating her breakfast—one Cheerio at a time. She doesn't have her hair brushed yet and the school bus is coming down the street.

Time to figure out what is causing the dawdling. Some children drag their feet in the morning because they are reluctant to go to school and aren't ready (or able) to articulate why. Maybe they're struggling in math or are being teased by the bigger kids on the bus. Fortunately most children dawdle simply because they're kids, and kids are still learning to grasp the concept of time.

If your child's dawdling is wreaking havoc on your nerves, try planning ahead. Everybody should do anything and everything they can the night before. For example, pack lunches or have milk money already on the counter. Make sure to have any papers or permission forms signed and ready to go. Doing what you can to take care of things the night before will make you less frazzled. And since children often reflect their parents' moods, chances are things will go more smoothly.

Have your child lay out the school clothes she wants to wear and track down her shoes. Also have your child put her homework in her backpack and put the backpack in a place where it'll be convenient to grab in a hurry. With older children, make it clear to your child that her things are her responsibility. If she forgets to put her clarinet, lunch, home-work, or gym shoes with her pile of things, you are not reminding her or bringing them to school during your lunch break.

If your child can barely tie his shoes, let alone find them the night before, get playful. Make getting ready for school a game. Ask, "Can you get your shoes on in under three minutes?"

or, "Can you find your library book by the time I sing the alphabet?" Putting on music may help dawdlers move faster—as long as they don't get distracted and start dancing, of course! Having a "no TV in the mornings" rule is also helpful when you have a distractible dawdler. Evoke your child's competitive spirit and challenge him to a race with you to get ready. But, no matter how tempting it is, don't challenge your children to race each other. You'll only be rolling out the red carpet for sibling rivalry.

Dealing with an older dawdler can be a bit more challenging. Nagging and yelling are like throwing gasoline on the fire, so appeal to your child's vanity. Let your child know you have no problem sending him to school in his pajamas if he doesn't get dressed in time. Remind him that not brushing his teeth will mean he has stinky breath all day and not combing his hair may mean he's the center of attention. Forgetting his gym shoes might mean he is the only one in the fourth grade who misses the big kickball game. And forgetting his lunch money will mean his stomach growls during afternoon silent-reading time. In other words, let your child suffer the natural consequences of not being ready on time. This is a great way to teach dawdlers to take responsibility for getting themselves ready.

A Rebel with a Cause (Or Dawdling for a Reason)

Face it. Some kids are homebodies. For these kids, not wanting to go to school is just part of their personalities, a quirk. There's also nothing to worry about when your child occasionally needs an extra hug or a few more minutes to ease into the day. If, however,

your normally easy-going child is clinging to you in the mornings or telling you he or she is lonesome for you during the school day, your "parent radar" should be pinging.

Unusual clinging or dawdling in the mornings can frequently be attributed to stress or emotional trauma. A new sibling, an accident, a bully, a death of a pet or grandparent, a family member's serious illness—all these things, along with countless other life events or daily stresses, can cause a child to suddenly drag his or her feet in the mornings or long for Mom or Dad during the school day. If your child or family has experienced an emotional event, take your cue from your child. Some kids will want to talk about their grief right away; others will stay bottled up for a few days. Some might be anxious to "get back to the routine," while others need a few days off. Be patient and generous with your time and comfort. Also, let your child's teacher know what's going on. This way she isn't caught off guard if your child suddenly bursts into tears in the middle of math.

Mountains and Molehills

"Oh, noooooo!" your child wails one morning. You jump out of bed and run down the hall to your child's bedroom, sure something awful has happened.

"What is it?" you demand.

"It's only Tuesday. I thought it was Wednesday," your daughter tells you. "I wanted to wear my purple dress but I have gym today and so I can't!"

Even though you might feel like throwing your hand against your chest and crying "You poor, poor thing!" try to refrain.

It's easy to forget what it's like to be a kid, when life's little snags—things that would be molehills to a grown-up—are mountains to kids. No, kids don't have to deal with mort-gage payments or the rising unemployment rate, but they do have real problems and it's important not to brush them off as trivial.

There are countless possible reasons your child may be dawdling in the mornings, or for that matter, coming home in a grumpy mood. Here are just a few you might consider: having to ride the bus, switching desks or table seats, forgetting a library book, his favorite shirt is in the dirty laundry, no snack in his lunchbox, having a substitute, having to give an oral report, not being picked for a team at recess, forgetting home-work, a favorite game or playground equipment already "taken," losing a lucky pencil, a pop quiz, not being invited to a birthday party, the teacher making a fuss over another child's essay and saying little about your child's work, or a friend who says he doesn't like your child anymore.

There are, of course, some children who are overly sensitive to life's daily surprises. For them, every problem is not just a moun-tain but Mount Everest! If your child is one of these kids, address the issue by suggesting she Stop, Step back, and Size up.

Stop. Tell your child that when she feels herself worrying about a problem, saying to herself, "Stop!" (or some other code word) will help keep anxiety from rising.

Step back. Have your child take a few deep breaths. This will calm her down and get her ready for the next step.

Size up. Ask your child to size up, or classify, the problem. Ask, "Will this problem be important tomorrow?" By asking whether a problem is worth all the energy she's expending, your child will gain a sense of control. And many times, just realizing she has control will give her confidence to tackle the problem.

COMMON SIGNS OF CHILDHOOD STRESS

Children, like adults, experience stress. While it's clear major events such as a new sibling or a divorce can be stressful, plenty of other things can be stressful for kids, too, like school pressures and bullying. Any behavior that is out of the ordinary for your child can be a sign of stress:

- *stomachaches without any other symptoms of illness*
- *frequent headaches*
- *sleeping too much or too little; loss of or increase in appetite.*
- *new habits such as hair twisting and nail biting*
- *new fears of the dark, monsters, or bad guys*
- *regression (for example, a ten-year-old suddenly starts sucking her thumb again)*
- *whining*
- *clinging or separation anxiety*
- *bedwetting or accidents*
- *withdrawing from family and friends*
- *bullying others or becoming defiant*

Showing one or two of these signs occasionally is no cause for alarm. However, if your child is showing several signs of stress or is showing signs frequently, it's time to act. The best thing a parent can do is open the lines of communication: take advantage of some quiet moments when the two of you are alone, just hanging out or doing something like taking a quick trip to the grocery store or playing a board game. Boys, especially, feel more comfortable opening up when they are involved with another activity. Be prepared for the floodgates to open at bedtime, too. Many kids use the peace and security they feel as Mom or Dad is tucking them in to talk about what's going on in their life. More often than not, children will feel better after expressing themselves. Listen to and validate your child's feelings but don't press. If things don't improve or your child seems depressed, don't hesitate to contact your pediatrician, school counselor, or another health expert.

Fake Stomachaches

I don't feel so good

It never fails. The morning you can't be late, your son drags himself downstairs and announces he has a stomachache and can't possibly be expected to go to school. You check his forehead. He doesn't feel warm, but he's giving his best performance ever. (The moaning alone is worthy of an Oscar.) You're pretty sure your son is faking, but the last time you sent him to school when you thought he was fine, he threw up in the middle of spelling. You waver. Then, you catch your son sneaking a donut. The jig is up.

The reasons children fake illnesses are as varied as children themselves. Like dawdling, faking a stomachache can be a sign a child is reluctant to go to school for a particular reason. (For example, your son knows there's going to be a substitute teacher.) It can also mean he is craving your attention or testing his boundaries. Or maybe there's just a movie on TV he wants to catch! Whatever the reason, there are several ways to deal with your "ill" child. What you choose to do depends on your child, your parenting style (or your mood), and maybe even your plans for the day.

Option one: Send him to school with sympathy. Occasionally, all that's needed to sooth an "upset stomach" is a few extra minutes of your time and a sympathetic ear. Give your son a hug, tell him you're sorry he's not feeling well, and that if he still isn't feeling well once he gets to school, you'll come get him. (You can also ask him to hang on until lunch.) Frequently, children will forget about their stomachaches after they meet up with friends and start their day.

Option two: Let him be a little late. Ever have a morning when you just can't seem to get motivated to move? Kids have those days, too. Maybe tummy trouble is your son's way of saying he needs a little more time, for whatever reason, to ease into the day. If it fits into your schedule, there's nothing wrong with letting your son miss the bus. As long as he understands it'll be a rare occurrence, this can be a good solution.

Option three: Let him stay home—with a twist (Part I). Let your son stay home and then make his day so boring that he'll be insisting he's made a miraculous recovery. Confine him to his bed and take away his television, radio, computer, and electronic games. If he complains, dump the contents of the sock basket on his bed and tell him to start sorting.

TO SEND 'EM OR NOT TO SEND 'EM— THAT IS THE DILEMMA

Your fifth-grader wakes up with a rash on his cheeks. He's not running a fever or acting ill and the rash isn't itchy. You go around and around. You know the school's policy is to send kids with unidentified rashes home, but your son's rash doesn't seem like that big a deal. In the end, you put him on the bus and say a prayer that if the school is going to call you to pick him up, they do it before you leave for yoga class.

It can be tricky to know when to send your "sort of sick" child to school. After all, maybe your son will perk up once he gets going or perhaps the touch of diarrhea was from something he ate. How sick is too sick to go to school? If your child exhibits any of the following, keep him home:

- *a temperature of 100 degrees or more*

- *vomiting or diarrhea within the last 24 hours*

- *excessive coughing or nasal discharge*

- *a rash with any other sign of illness*

- *a moderate or severe sore throat*

- *any sign of a contagious illness such as pink eye, chicken pox, lice, etc.*

An ill child should be kept at home until he or she has been fever-free and/or has taken any prescribed antibiotics for 24 hours.

Option four: Let him stay home—with a twist (Part II). Let your son get comfortable on the couch or in his bed and then watch him like a hawk. The minute there's any sign of improvement (for example, he asks to watch TV), pack him up and drag him into school. Feel free to use the ever-popular line, "If you're well enough to watch TV, you're well enough to go to school!" This approach, as well as the one right above, lets your child know he'd better be prepared to get what he asks for.

Option five: Send him to school with no sympathy. This is not so much the "tough love" approach as it's the "tough luck" approach. Tell your son you know he's faking and he's going to school. End of discussion. If you have time, you can always throw in the "boy who cried wolf" speech.

Heavy Backpacks

Back in your day, you had to walk to school (uphill, both ways) and carry all your books and supplies in your arms. Nowadays, kids lug their belongings on their backs, and there's growing concern that the convenience of backpacks is coming at the cost of good health. Consistently carrying around a backpack that is too heavy has been linked to back, shoulder, and neck fatigue and strain, as well as headaches. Heavy backpacks can also cause pulled muscles or slipped discs when children try to yank them up too quickly.

HOW HEAVY IS TOO HEAVY?

Body strength, build, and overall health play a part in how much weight your child can comfortably carry. But the American Academy of Pediatrics recommends that your child's backpack be limited to ten to twenty percent of his or her bodyweight.

To reduce the weight your child carries each day, first help him or her remove unnecessary items. In other words, is the rock collection really essential? How about the skateboard or the three library books? (The books are probably overdue, anyway.) Try to reduce the load so that the backpack can pass the one-hand test. In other words, your child should be able to lift the backpack using only one hand.

So how can you help reduce the odds that your child will be a victim of a "backpack attack?" First and foremost, make sure your child's backpack is the right size. Don't buy an oversized backpack so your child can grow into it. If the straps are up by your child's ears or the pack hangs below his or her behind, the backpack is too big.

As shocking as it might be to kids, backpacks should be worn on the back. Too often, children simply sling heavy packs over a shoulder. This practice can strain shoulder and neck muscles. In addition to wearing both straps (which, ideally, should be padded), children need to use the hip strap if one is available. (Many inexpensive backpacks do not come with a hip strap.) The strap should fit tightly around your child, just above his hips so the bulk of the weight is resting there. Shoulder straps should be pulled snug and any extra straps need to be shortened or secured so they don't catch on anything (like a closing bus or car door). Children should pack heavier items first so that they are close to their backs. This helps distribute weight better and consequently prevents your kindergartner from tipping over backwards and getting stuck like an upside down turtle.

Last-Minute Surprises

They're the kind of words that strike fear in the heart of a mother: "Mom, I just remembered I signed up to bring cupcakes to the party and it's today."

Oh, if only I had known about this last night, you think. Not that you had all the necessary ingredients or even the energy to bake cupcakes from scratch.

It's inevitable. Your child is going to spring a few last-minute surprises on you during her grade school career. Some might be as easy as needing a signature on a permission slip or a couple of dollars to buy a new pencil at the school supply store. Others may be as stressful as, "Sorry, I forgot. The principal wants to have a conference this morning." When you're hit with the unexpected, the first rule is "Don't panic." Stop, take a deep breath, think, and make a mental note to give the lecture later. There are really only two ways to deal with a last-minute surprise.

First, you can do your best. Scrounge around for loose change or raid a piggy bank. (Pennies aren't pretty, but they'll do in a pinch if your child needs field trip money.) Your turn to bring snack? Combine all those nearly-empty cereal boxes to make trail mix or swing by the store to buy cupcakes. Then remind yourself the world and your status as a good parent will not end if you bring store-bought treats. You can also ask a neighbor for help. You'd be surprised by what some of your friends have tucked in their pantries or junk drawers. And most parents are happy to help out, knowing their turn to scramble is coming.

INSIDER TIP

Many schools and teachers are now online. Ask your child's teacher if he has an email address and provide yours. This will allow you to touch base with your child's teacher with any questions you have about upcoming, important dates and your child's teacher can easily send out reminders via email.

INSIDER TIP

Some environmentally minded schools send papers home with just one child in each family. This practice may help save trees, but it sometimes means important notices are not finding their way to your house. If your school has a policy of sending PTO fliers or other school-wide announcements home with just one child, ask that the papers be sent with your most reliable child. If you have only one child and he or she somehow manages to lose important papers in the fifteen minutes between the time he or she leaves school and walks inside the house, ask the school to consider sending papers home on a certain day. Having a designated day for school-home correspondence will help both parents and children. Suggesting to your child's school that important announcements be on bright paper might help too. For example, if you spy a hot pink piece of paper shoved in the corner of your child's backpack you'll know it's important.

When it comes to last-minute surprises, the best defense is a good offense. Keeping track of upcoming events, deadlines, or papers that need to be filled out can greatly reduce the number of last-minute surprises and the anxiety they bring. Some families hang a large calendar in a central location to record everyone's schedules and To Do lists. Other families use a bulletin board or a Dry Erase board. Have an "in box" or an "all points bulletin" board or some other designated spot for important papers. Make it a family rule that notes from school are taken out of backpacks and put in the spot (or handed to Mom or Dad) immediately after arriving home. Consider having an "out box" or basket where you put notes to teachers, volunteer sign-ups, and other papers that need to go back to school. Put the basket next to the door you leave by in the morning. Help your child get into the habit of checking the box before putting on his or her jacket and backpack. The secret is to find an organization system that works for your family and use it.

On the Way to School

Fear of the School Bus

It's the first day of school, and your kindergartner has been up and dressed since 6:00. "Is it time yet?" she asks every five minutes. Finally, the two of you walk to the bus stop and visit with the other children and parents waiting there. Soon the big, yellow bus makes the turn and rumbles down the street. When the bus stops and opens its doors, the other children climb the stairs confidently. But not your daughter. "I'm not getting on that thing!" she announces.

Fear of riding a school bus is not uncommon. The same friendly looking buses that make parents jump up and down with joy can make some children panic. School buses are big, boxy, noisy, and driven by an unfamiliar face. No wonder some kids are apprehensive. If she hasn't had a chance to do so already, arrange for your child to take a tour of a school bus. On the first day of school, be sure to introduce your child to the bus driver. If you are allowed on the bus (and your child is reasonably calm and doesn't have a death grip on you), help her find a seat on the first day. Just be sure to say good-bye and make a quick exit because the longer you linger, the more apprehensive your child may become.

Some children are concerned that the bus will tip over in a crash. Reassure your child the odds of being in an accident are quite small and the odds of tipping over are even smaller. Encourage her to find a seat close to the driver or beside a friend. Consider enlisting the help of an older sibling or child from the neighborhood to be a "bus buddy" for a week or two.

Because they are large, heavy, highly visible, and distribute crash force differently than other vehicles, school buses are

statistically very safe. Since the early 1970s, school buses have used the compartmentalization approach to rider safety. Seats are higher, reinforced, well padded, and close together so that in a crash, kids are kept safe in a "compartment." Several studies have suggested that adding seat belts would not greatly improve this system and may even be more dangerous.

"Is This the Right Bus?"

Getting on the right bus is usually pretty easy in the mornings. Go to your bus stop. Wait. And when a bus comes, get on it. But the afternoons are a different story. Suppose everyone drove the same model and color car. Can you imagine how confusing it would be to locate your vehicle in a crowded parking lot? This is what it can feel like to a child trying to find his or her bus after school. Especially if he or she is prone to mixing up 14 and 41. Rest assured, schools and transportation departments have procedures to get kids on the right bus. How can parents help? Here are a few tips:

- Find out your child's bus number ahead of time and make sure your child knows it. Help your child find a memory aid, such as a rhyme. For example, "When school is done, go to bus forty-one!"

- Help your child write his name and bus number on a piece of paper and keep it pinned on the inside of his backpack.

- Teach your child to look for familiar faces when she climbs on the bus. If she doesn't recognize the driver or other riders, tell her to ask the driver for help.

- Ask your child's school about putting a simple picture (for example, a dog or sun) under the number for early readers. This way, young students have two ways to identify their bus.

Safety at the Bus Stop

Whether your child waits alone, with other children, or with you at the bus stop, go over these basic safety rules and review them frequently:

Be on time. When children run late, the odds of getting careless—running out in the street or between parked cars—increases.

Be extra careful when crossing the street. People are more apt to be in a hurry in the mornings. This means speeding cars and distracted drivers. Also warn your child that the glare of the rising sun can cause vehicles to have blind spots. They should never assume that a driver can see them just because they can see the driver.

Stop at driveways. Rushing commuters may back up without looking so teach your child to always stop at the edge of any driveway before crossing.

Stay away from the curb. While at the bus stop, children should wait several feet away from the curb. Standing too close to the road is dangerous because your child might be pushed or accidentally trip into the street. Being close to the road also means your child would be within arm's reach of a stranger pulling up alongside the curb.

INSIDER TIP

Let your child's teacher know if your child is getting himself on the bus in the mornings. This way, if your child doesn't show up as expected, the school can notify you right away. If you don't let them know, school personnel may think your child is ill or running late and you simply haven't called yet.

Keep backpacks on. Removing backpacks at the bus stop and setting them down to run around causes a tripping hazard.

Stay at the bus stop. Going back for forgotten items is a no-no; when you hurry, you're more likely to forget the rules and take careless chances.

Wait with someone you know. If possible, your child should wait with a sibling or a friend. He or she should also know the names of any adults who are at the bus stop so they can tell them if an older kid starts bothering them.

Be patient. When the bus pulls up, your child should wait until it comes to a complete stop and the driver has opened the door and given the okay signal to board. Remind your child to hold the rails and don't push in line.

Stay away from the bus's rear wheels at all times. The back wheel area of a bus is a very dangerous spot because the driver cannot see them well. Children should never cross behind the bus to get to the bus stop or to go home.

Too Late! Missing the Bus

Sometimes, no matter how fast your child moves or how much you holler "Hurry up!" luck is just not on your side. Like a last-minute snow day announcement, a missed school bus can throw a household for a loop. How you handle this snafu largely depends on your family routine.

First and foremost, any child who rides a school bus should be instructed as to where to go if he or she misses the bus. Make it an iron-clad rule your child either comes straight home or goes to another designated place. Remind your child NEVER to accept a ride from a stranger or even from someone he knows. Accepting a ride from a friend without your permission is not a good idea since the school is expecting your child on the bus. What if the ride gets a flat tire or is delayed by a train, or stops for a last-minute errand? If your child doesn't get off as expected and the school calls you, everyone is going to panic.

If someone is home when your child misses the bus, you and your child have a few options. Because you want your child to be ultimately responsible for getting ready and getting to the bus stop on time, using natural consequences is the best response. What would be the natural consequences of missing the school bus? The obvious one is for your child to walk or ride his bike to school, even if that means he is late. Of course, walking to school may not be a practical solution if distance or weather is a factor. In this case, you might consider driving your child to school and charging him for your "taxi services." If your child doesn't have allowance money, take the payment in time. For example, if it takes you ten minutes to drive your child to school, have your child spend ten minutes in his room or do ten minutes worth of extra chores after school.

If no one is home when your child misses the bus, options are a little more limited. Plan A should be for your child to go to a pre-determined safe place, such as a neighbor's house or a store. From there, your child can call you and you can make the necessary arrangements to get him to school. Since Plan A may not always work, give your child a Plan B or even a Plan C! For example, if no one is home at the designated place (How dare your neighbor go on vacation and not tell you!), instruct your child to go straight home and wait.

If you live fairly close to school, your child can always implement Plan C—walking to school. Tell your child that if he decides to walk he needs to take the route the two of you have agreed on. No short cuts! This way, you or school personnel can travel the route, looking for your child if he doesn't arrive when expected.

Whoops! "What If My Child Doesn't Get Off Where He's Supposed To?"

It's the end of the day and you're a little late getting to the bus stop. Children are pouring off the bus. You wait at the end of your driveway and look for your child. And look. And look. Pretty soon,

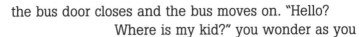

the bus door closes and the bus moves on. "Hello? Where is my kid?" you wonder as you take off on foot. (Who knew you could still run that fast?) After chasing down the bus, you discover your child is safely on board. She just missed her stop.

As bad as it feels to watch the bus pull away with your child still on it, it's much worse for the child who suddenly realizes she missed her stop. If your child is worried about missing the stop and you're not able to meet her in the afternoons with a giant "Exit Bus Now" sign, there are several things you can do.

First, get in your car some afternoon and travel the bus route with your child. Show her landmarks like big trees or a house with a boulder in the yard that she can use to keep track of where she is. Another trick is to count off each stop so that your child can keep track while she's riding. ("The bus stops five times and then I get off.") If counting stops is too challenging, consider setting an alarm on a wristwatch. It doesn't have to be exact; it just has to warn your child to start paying attention.

Second, tell your child to keep an eye out for the kids she knows get off at her stop. (Your child's bus driver will also have a list of who gets off where.) Having several people to watch for is better than having just one friend since an absent buddy could throw the whole plan off and your bus rider into an anxiety attack.

And finally, plan for the worst. Reassure your child that if she forgets

INSIDER TIP

To save valuable minutes (and your sanity) when your child doesn't get off at the right bus stop, track down the bus transportation department's phone number ahead of time and either post it or carry it with you. This is an especially wise idea in case your school doesn't answer the phone after school.

PLANNING FOR THE UNEXPECTED

Last-minute school cancellations or early dismissals due to weather or other emergencies happen. Schools make every effort to announce these situations through the media, but they simply cannot call every parent and make sure someone will be home for each child. For this reason, it's best to be prepared. Schools generally send home a form designating where your bus rider should be dropped off in the event of an emergency. (Or where your "walker" should go.) Watch for this form in the fall. If you don't get one, make sure you follow up or insist that the school implement an early dismissal policy.

Go over this form with your child and make sure she knows where to go if school should be unexpectedly dismissed early. (For example, "If school gets out early and I'm not home, go to Sam's house or Kim's house.") It's also a good idea to let your child know who is on your "emergency phone numbers" list and anybody who you have given school written permission to pick her up in the event you cannot be reached. These preparations are also important in the event you are unable to make it home in time to meet the bus.

to get off at the right stop, no one will be mad and the bus driver will get her home. Role-play with your child so she can practice telling the bus driver what's happened as well as recite her address.

And if you can't catch up with the bus at the next stop or two, call the bus transportation department. (The school should have the number if you can't find it. Sometimes the school can even radio the bus for you.) This goes for when your child doesn't show up at the babysitter's house or friend's house as expected. Give your child's bus number and explain the situation. The dispatcher can radio the driver for you. Most of the time, the driver will have to finish her route before taking your child home.

"You Heard WHAT on the Bus?"

You and your neighbor are enjoying a pleasant visit when your first grader comes into the room with your friend's toddler in tow. "Mom, look what I taught the baby!" she says as she holds up the

"YOU DID **WHAT** ON THE BUS?"

With only one adult to supervise the entire bus, it's not surprising there are occasional problems; it might be surprising, though, when it's your child who is acting up on the school bus! To help mornings and afternoons go smoothly for everyone, make sure your bus rider knows the rules, and understands that riding the bus is a privilege that can be taken away. Common infractions that might get your child a warning or a suspension from the bus include: fighting at the bus stop, using the wrong bus stop, using foul language or rude gestures, creating excessive noise or rough-housing, moving or standing up when the bus is in motion, throwing things out the window, carrying a weapon or hazardous material of any kind, using emergency exits in a non-emergency situation, and disrespecting or disobeying the bus driver.

If your child has been caught acting inappropriately on the school bus, ask for details from the bus driver, witnesses, and your child. Unless your child is obviously being treated unfairly, support any decision by the bus department as far as discipline action goes. Let your child feel the natural consequences of his or her actions. This may mean she must walk or ride a bike to school while sus-pended from the bus. It may also mean that she has to reimburse you (or another driver) for taking her to and from school. This reimbursement may be in the form of money or time.

other child's middle finger. "She's shooting the bird!" You want to crawl under the table and your friend suddenly remembers she has to get home right away.

"Where did you learn that?" you ask your child.

"From some big kids on the bus," she tells you.

Because a large cross-section of students and students of varying ages ride together on school buses, it's highly likely, at some point, your child will hear or see something you wish they wouldn't. Here are some ways to handle it when it happens:

Remain calm. Of course, it can be disturbing to hear swear words come out of your child's mouth or see him or her doing crude gestures, but don't overreact! If your child is young, he probably doesn't understand the words or gestures and is just mimicking what he has seen; if your child is older, he may just be trying to get a reaction. Either way, it's best to respond calmly.

Let your child know exactly what word or which behavior is unacceptable. Make your feelings clear. In a no-nonsense tone, tell your child, "We don't use that word in our family," or "That gesture is hurtful to other people's feelings. Don't use it."

Give your child alternatives. Let him or her know what words he or she could use instead. For example, "Oh, fiddlesticks!" or "Shoot fire!" are silly-sounding but acceptable.

Give your child solutions. Of course, telling your child not to use certain words or gestures and offering alternatives will not keep him or her from hearing or seeing inappropriate things on the bus. Empower your child by encouraging her to sit with friends her age and away from the offending kids. Suggest that she hum softly or look away if other kids are being rude. Role play with

your child so he or she can practice saying, "I don't like that word. Stop using it around me!" to someone being rude.

Step in if necessary. If the bad language or behavior is harmful or ongoing, you need to step in. Busses, likes schools, have a zero-tolerance policy when it comes to violence or sexual harassment. Contact the school immediately. Ask to see their transportation policy and request that your child's bus be equipped with a video camera and begin to document any inappropriate language or behavior yourself. Keep a journal with the date and a detailed description of any poor or harmful

WHAT IF THE BUS DRIVER IS MEAN OR INCOMPETENT?

In a perfect world, all bus drivers would have a big smile for children every day and faithfully obey all the rules of the road. Unfortunately, mean and incompetent bus drivers are around. If your child complains about having to ride the bus or tells you his or her bus driver is mean (or you've witnessed a worrisome incident), how you can respond depends on a few factors.

If the bus driver is verbally or physically abusive or is blatantly ignoring inappropriate behavior on the bus or at the bus stop, you have a responsibility to contact the school transportation department and report the driver. Do not hesitate to make other arrangements for getting your child to and from school; your child must know you're doing your job of keeping her safe.

If your child's bus driver is just an unpleasant person and you're not willing or able to drive your child to school, tell your child she doesn't have to grin, but she might just have to bear it. If there are no assigned seats, suggest to your child that he sit as far away from the bus driver as possible. Your child might try "killing the driver with kindness" or finding at least one likeable thing about the driver to focus on and see if that helps. If nothing else, you can always remind your child he has to put up with the sourpuss for only a short time each day.

behavior your child has reported.

Carpools

Many areas don't have school buses. What's a busy parent to do when school and work schedules (or baby's sleep schedule) don't mesh? Carpooling may be just the answer.

When setting up a carpool, you need to consider three things: proximity, flexibility, and compatibility. After all, how much time are you going to save if you have to drive across town to pick up a rider or if another driver can never drive on Mondays, Wednesdays, or Fridays? And how happy are you and your child going to be if one of the carpool parents (or his or her child) is someone the two of you can't stand?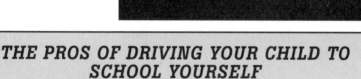

Size is another important factor when consider-

THE PROS OF DRIVING YOUR CHILD TO SCHOOL YOURSELF

The benefits include:

- *even short trips to and from school can give parent and child a great opportunity to talk or simply to be together*

- *no extra kids means less chaos and a calmer start to the day for both of you*

- *you get to work around your own schedule, so on a crazy morning there's less anxiety because your child is the only one late to school*

- *no carpool responsibilities if you're on vacation or sick*

- *you know your child is with a safe driver!*

ing or setting up a carpool. You want a carpool to be big enough that there is some flexibility but small enough to be safe. Typically, carpools with three to four riders work well. For safety reasons, parents must remember to include siblings in this count. Every child needs a seat with a seat belt (and a car seat or booster seat if applicable), and no young child should be seated in the front with the driver.

Once you've come up with a carpool, your group needs to designate a main contact or head driver. This is the person who should be called in an emergency or who will make a decision about carpool in poor weather conditions. This person should also provide each driver with a list of the children, their addresses, and emergency information (such as age, allergies, medical history, and parents' names and phone numbers). *THIS LIST SHOULD BE IN EACH CAR EACH CARPOOL DAY.* If the unthinkable happens, it's important for emergency personnel to have this information.

The next thing parents need to do is set up some ground rules. As a group, agree how these things will be handled: car or medical emergencies, bad behavior, bad language, appropriate topics of conversation, appropriate radio stations or CD's, sick or vacationing driver or carpooler, tardiness, eating in the car, nobody at home when child is dropped off, running errands along the way, a carpooler bringing home a friend, or being dropped off at a friend's house.

Chapter 3

The Teacher From the Black Lagoon: Snafus in the Classroom

Y ou've finally got your children up, fed, dressed, and loaded in the van. You can see the light at the end of the tunnel and are starting to relax a bit as you turn into the drop-off lane in front of school. What could possibly go wrong now?

Uh . . . don't ask.

"My teacher hates me!" your daughter wails as the car comes to a stop. "And there's going to be a fire drill today! And I have to give my report in front of the whole class this afternoon!"

You fumble around, trying to decide which problem needs addressing first. After several minutes, hugs, some off-the-cuff advice, and a promise to talk about everything later, your daughter feels better. She climbs out of the van. You turn and look at your fifth grader, "So. Do you have any complaints you'd like to register?"

"Yeah," he says. "I only get five minutes to eat lunch."

That reminds you—your kids' lunchboxes are still sitting on the kitchen counter.

Teachers, Children, and Parents

When a Child and Teacher Don't Click

It's only the second week of school and already your son has a note from the principal. "It says here you were caught drawing this unflattering picture of your teacher," you say, glancing at the attached caricature (which you, being the unbiased person you are, have to admit is pretty good).

"It's not my fault!" your son yells. "Mr. Stewart is the creature from the Black Lagoon. He hates me!"

Wouldn't it be wonderful if your child loved all of his teachers and all his teachers adored him? Of course it would. But, unfortunately, you live in a little place called the Real World. In the Real World, students and teachers some-times don't like each other. Chances are good that at some point, your child is going to come across a teacher with whom he just does-n't click. How can parents help?

Don't panic. Despite schools' best efforts to match students and teachers, personality clashes happen. (Many schools have parents fill out personality questionnaires about their children.) All is not lost;

your child is not destined to have a terrible school year just because his teacher is not his all-time favorite. It may take effort, but all parties involved can work through this problem. Don't forget to consider that the discord could be temporary. Maybe your child just needs more time to warm up to the new teacher and her teaching style.

Listen to your child but assume nothing. Try to find out what exactly is happening in the classroom. Did the teacher do something specific that upset your child or made him feel as if he was picked on? Dig for details. Did the teacher call him a name? Did she tell your son to put his work away before he had a chance to finish it? Ask your child to describe the teacher's interactions in the classroom. Is the new teacher's style different than your child's previous teacher's style? (For example, some teachers are yellers while others are soft-spoken; some are all business while others like to joke around.) Asking your child how the teacher treats other kids in the classroom can also give you insight into the situation. Does your child feel singled out or is everyone having a hard time with the "mean teacher?" Of course you want to believe your child, but his is only one side of the story. For example, maybe your child was given ten extra minutes to complete his work before the teacher made him put it away.

Meet with the teacher. Bring an open mind, not an attitude. This is an opportunity to see for yourself what the teacher is like and to hear his or her interpretation of events. Be prepared to talk about specific incidents your child has shared with you. This is also a good time to fill in the teacher on your child's personality or any strategies you've found successful with your child. For example, you know your child needs several warnings, not just one or two, so he can transition to a new lesson or activity smoothly.

When a Child and Teacher Still Don't Click

Ok, so you've met the teacher and you've discovered that he is, in fact, the creature from the Black Lagoon. Now what? If a personality clash is making school completely unbearable for your child:

Ask for a meeting with the teacher and the principal.
Principals are supportive of their staff but they are committed to meeting the needs of students and their parents, as well. Having a third, objective party involved is a good idea if the parent-teacher conference has gotten you nowhere. Perhaps the principal will have some valuable insight. At the very least, he or she will be aware of the problem and may take a more active role in your child's classroom, monitoring the situation or being a friendly face for your child. It can also be helpful to include your child's guidance counselor.

Request a transfer. If it's early in the school year, transferring to another classroom might be a good solution. (If it's late in the year, schools will most likely suggest your child finish out the year or do home study.) Be prepared for resistance, though. Many principals don't want to set a precedent.

Prepare for the long haul. If a transfer isn't possible or is something you don't want to do, sit down with your child and come up with a plan for the year. Don't blame your child or his teacher; explain that sometimes, people just don't get along. Help your child see that he can help the situation by avoiding certain hot-button issues. For example, if you know your son's teacher has a thing about neatness, your son can make sure his homework is legible. Perhaps your child and teacher could write and sign a contract highlighting a few goals your child will work on and how he will meet those goals. This will show your child's teacher that your child is genuinely trying and the effort might be enough to ease tensions. Volunteering in your child's classroom will let you keep an eye on things and let your child know you support him.

Prepare for next year. Having a teacher he doesn't get along with can be extremely stressful for your child. But having two teachers in a row he doesn't click with can be crushing and turn him off of school altogether. Don't let this happen. As a parent, you must be proactive and plan for the following year. Most schools honor requests from parents who want their child to be in a certain teacher's class or with a certain type of teacher if they have valid concerns. Begin thinking about what type of classroom environment your child will need next year and write a letter to the right person. (This is often the school counselor.)

Teacher's Pets

No matter what your child may believe, teachers are human. They're going to respond better to some students than they do to others. It's natural. Most teachers are careful to keep their personal feelings out of the classroom. But every once in awhile, they fail.

It can be difficult for parents to know what goes on in their children's classroom all day long. There are a few things that might indicate your child's teacher is playing favorites either with certain students or with a particular gender. The biggest tip-off is if you repeatedly hear things from your child, their friends, and other parents. For example, the teacher accepts late work from a particular student (when the policy is to not accept it), calls only on the girls (or boys), is more demanding or lenient of certain children, always gives certain kids the "good jobs" like line leader, or has talked about a child to another child's parent in a negative way. You may even observe favoritism when you volunteer in the classroom or on field trips.

If Your Child Feels Slighted

Let your child know she has done nothing wrong and is a likeable person. When she stamps her foot and complains it's not fair that the teacher seems to like so-and-so better, tell her she's right! It isn't fair.

Bring the offending behavior to the teacher's attention. Many times, just making the teacher aware of what she is doing and how it's affecting the students will put an end to it.

If the favoritism is an on-going problem and you've tried talking to the teacher with no results, talk to the principal. Be ready to discuss specific incidents.

If Your Child is the Teacher's Pet

Bring the favoritism to the teacher's attention. Even if it's your child who's being singled out in a favorable way, this kind of behavior needs to be addressed.

Just like they know who's in what reading group, kids are keenly aware who the teacher likes best. If your child is getting special treatment or even if other kids just think your child is getting special treatment, they may fight back. Watch for signs your child is being teased or bullied.

Don't let your child use her honored place in her teacher's heart to slack off or act up. Hold her to high standards even if the teacher doesn't.

Great Parent-Teacher Conferences

You've heard horror stories about conferences from you-know-where. (Your friends went to a conference where the teacher accidentally spent the first ten minutes talking about another

---

YOU DON'T LIKE YOUR CHILD'S TEACHER

What if your child adores his new teacher, but YOU can't stand her? Whatever you do, don't bad mouth the teacher in front of your child or in front of other parents. This undermines the teacher's authority and can cause your child to question his or her feelings. ("Hmm. Mom doesn't like Mrs. Kelly, maybe I shouldn't either.") Try to find something you like about the teacher. She makes great bulletin boards, she reads to the kids every day, she wears clothes that match—there must be at least one positive thing you can say about your child's teacher.

Try to give her a chance. Your second impression may be better than the first. And finally, if all else fails just remember it's your child who's in the classroom all day, not you! Does it really matter if you can't stand the teacher?

INSIDER TIP

Keep an ear open when you're driving your child and his or her friends around or when they are hanging out together. You can gather a great deal of information about what's going on in the classroom this way—information your child may not otherwise share. Keep your ears open at school functions and sports activities, too. Listen to what other parents are saying about what's happening to their children or what they see in the classroom.

student!) Or maybe the idea of sitting down with a teacher takes you back to your own school days and makes you as nervous as a kid on report-card day. How can you help make parent-teacher conferences go smoothly and be productive?

First, talk to your child before you go. If you haven't already, ask her what her favorite part of the day is or what she likes best about school. Ask if there's anything she doesn't like about school or is having trouble with. Is there anything your child wants you to bring up with her teacher? Let your child know you and her teacher aren't going to spend the time tattling or telling embarrassing stories about her! Reassure her you and the teacher are just working together to make sure she is having a good school year.

Second, be prepared. Show up a few minutes early so you're not rushed and can look at any artwork or projects your child has hanging out in the hall. Bring your student if you'd like to include them, but if possible, leave siblings at home; they can be distracting. (Even good-natured toddlers and sleeping babies can quickly become distracting.) Bring a list of questions you'd like to ask or make an outline of things you want to make sure to cover. In addition, if you haven't done so already, make sure you've looked over your child's interim report or report card and work he or she has brought home recently so you know how your child is doing in school.

Greet the teacher warmly. He will most likely have a long list of parents to see and will appreciate a kind word. Besides, if you have a complaint, "pouncing" on the teacher immediately will probably put him on the defensive. Since you'll have a short amount of time to cover a lot of ground, keep chitchat to a minimum. Ask specific questions. Take notes if you need to. Be an active listener. Be sure to bring up any questions or concerns you or your child has.

At the end of the conference, ask the teacher if another conference is needed to further discuss a concern. When you get home, share what you can about the conference with your child. It can be nerve-racking to know someone has been talking about you!

When Teachers Leave Mid-Year

Your daughter comes home in tears one afternoon. "Today I heard the worst news ever! Mrs. Denny is having a baby!"

You're a little confused why a baby is bad news until your child adds, "And she's leaving the class forever after Thanksgiving!"

Life happens. Teachers have babies or a change of heart about their careers. They are offered other jobs or have spouses who are transferred. They get sick, hurt, and unfortunately, sometimes pass away.

Whether or not the teacher's departure is planned or unexpected, the most important thing you can do for your child is let her grieve over the loss in her own way. Saying good-bye to someone you like and having the dynamics in your classroom shift can be tough on kids, especially for those who are sensitive to change. Your child may begin to act out in class or at home. She may cry or be reluctant to go to school. She may even begin to bad-mouth her beloved teacher, saying things like "I didn't like Mrs. Denny anyway! I'm glad she's leaving." This is a defense mechanism, a way for your child to distance herself from the teacher and make the break easier. It's best to stand back and let your child vent. Let her know that, when she's ready, you'll be there to listen or give her a hug.

If it's at all possible, help your child say good-bye to his or her teacher because doing so can give children a sense of closure. This good-bye can be as formal as a card, letter, picture, or small gift, or as informal as a hug on the teacher's last day. If the teacher's departure was sudden, due to illness or death, you might have to be a bit more resourceful. Encourage your child to send the teacher a Get Well card or plant a tree or some flowers in the teacher's memory. Depending on your child's age and the circumstances, you may want to consider taking your child to the teacher's memorial service. Contact the school's counselor or your child's pediatrician for further advice.

Children are great at picking up and reflecting their parents' feelings so be enthusiastic about the new teacher. Don't complain or use negative words like "upheaval" or "mess." Your child may be worried about what the new teacher will be like. Let her know her teacher probably got to help pick out who's replacing her and she wouldn't pick someone who was mean! Focus on the positives and your child will, too. Don't be surprised, though, if your

10 Ways To Be the Kind of Parent Teachers Brag About

Parents like to brag about their children's great teachers. Guess what. It works both ways! When there are positive feelings on both sides of the desk, everyone wins—especially your child. So what does it take to be the kind of parent that teachers rave about?

1. Make sure your child comes to school ready to learn. This means a good night's sleep and a healthy breakfast.

2. Show your child's teacher respect. Address her by her title and last name (unless otherwise instructed) and speak to her with kindness.

3. Stand behind the teacher's decisions. Even when you don't agree with a teacher's action, it's important to back her up. To do otherwise only undermines her authority in the class and with your child.

4. Have an open mind. Your child's teacher may have a unique approach in the classroom. Different does not automatically mean bad.

5. Volunteer! Teachers and students love for parents to help.

6. Ask questions. If you are confused or concerned about something, don't hesitate to approach your child's teacher. Don't let things simmer until you or your child is really unhappy.

7. Read to your child daily. Even children who know how to read themselves benefit from being read to.

8. Be tuned in to what your child is working on at school. Know when homework or projects are due or when tests or special events are coming up.

9. Make education a priority. Children learn by watching so make sure your actions show how important you think it is to get a good education. This might mean turning off the television each night so your child can do his or her homework or not taking unnecessary vacations during the school year.

10. Sign notes, permission slips, report cards, and other forms right away. It may sound simple, but parents make things a lot easier for teachers when they respond quickly to papers that are sent home!

child spends a lot of time talking about the old teacher for a while. (Some children will also express themselves by drawing pictures or engaging in pretend play.) This doesn't mean your child is unhappy or doesn't like the new teacher; this may just be her way of processing what's happened.

Fears and Behavior in the Classroom

When Your Child Is Afraid of Emergency Drills

It's early evening and you're picking up your child from the after school program. "How was your day?" you ask as the two of you head toward the car.

"Terrible! I never want to go back to school!" your child declares.

With some gentle probing, you discover the reason your child has decided to be a grade-school dropout is that there was a fire drill during the day. Apparently, the whole thing threw your child for a loop.

Kid-pleasing or not, safety drills are a part of school life. Fire drills, inclement weather drills, security lockdown drills and, where needed, earthquake drills, are required by law in schools. They are in place to protect children, but some children don't find them comforting! How can you help your drill dodger?

First, explain why drills are important. Tell your child that in emergencies, people sometimes panic and forget where to go and what to do and practicing helps everyone remain calm. Compare emergency drills to practicing a sport or studying for a test. Your child might feel better if he or she can see value in the drills. Then again, your child may not really care why drills are done. (The younger your child, the less likely he or she will be placated by explanations.) In this case, simply tell your child it's the rule his school has drills. Having to follow rules is something all kids can relate to.

RELAXATION TECHNIQUES FOR KIDS

Besides taking deep breaths and using positive self-talk, there are other ways for your child to calm herself down during an emergency or a drill. Children can try any of the following:

Hum quietly. *Remind your child it's important to hum as quietly as possible so she can hear the teacher give instructions.*

Stretch. *Encourage your child to stretch her hands overhead if it's safe to do so.*

Blow the stress away. *This is a good variation of deep breathing if your child is really tense. Have your child inhale through the nose until the lungs are full, then open her mouth and let the air rush out.*

Shrug their shoulders. *This action helps release stress in the shoulders, neck, and back.*

Think of a happy picture. *Tell your child to remember a happy place or time or think of something that makes her happy. Remind your child to keep his or her eyes open, though. Closed eyes are not useful in an emergency!*

Smile. *Explain to your child that he can trick himself into feeling better by pretending he already does by smiling.*

Rub their hands together. *Rubbing your hands together softly is a quiet way to release nervous energy.*

Say the alphabet in their heads. *Reciting something familiar will give your child something to focus on (other than her fear) without distracting her from the teacher.*

Next, prepare your child for drills. It varies in each state how many drills are required throughout the school year, although most schools are required by law to conduct fire drills monthly. Many schools give teachers and students warning before sounding an alarm, either in the morning or a few minutes before. If your child knows the drill is coming, he can prepare himself mentally. Encourage your child to take several deep breaths and think, "I'm okay. This is only a drill." Suggest

RESOURCES TO CHECK OUT

For more information on how to prepare for an emergency or how to help your child prepare or deal with one, try one of these resources.

American Psychological
Association
750 First Street, NE
Washington, DC 20002
(800) 374-2721
www.apa.org

American Red Cross
National Headquarters
2025 E. Street, NW
Washington, DC 20006
(202) 303-4498
www.redcross.org

Federal Emergency
Management Agency (FEMA)
www.fema.gov

National Association of
School Psychologists
4340 East West Highway,
Suite 402
Bethesda, MD 20814
(301) 657-0270
www.nasponline.org

National Center for
Post-Traumatic Stress Disorder
VA Medical Center
215 North Main Street
White River Junction, VT 05001
(802) 296-6300
www.ncptsd.org/facts/specifics/
fschildren.html

to your child he close his eyes and think about what he's going to do and where he's going to go when the alarm rings or the announcement to "lock down" comes. Visualization is a great tool children can use to gain a sense of control over themselves and their environment.

Next, acknowledge and validate your child's fears. Let her know it's okay to be afraid sometimes. Ask your daughter what specifically she's afraid of. Is it the sound of the alarm that's bothering her? Is she worried she'll get separated from her class during a drill? Is she claustrophobic and nervous about squeezing under a table or in a small space? Pinpointing what is most worrisome is helpful because just naming the fear can take away much of its power. Just be careful not to let your child dwell on his or her fears; this only heightens anxiety again.

And finally, because children can sense and react to their parents' stress, do what you can to downplay your own fears. This includes your concerns about lockdowns and other security drills that were not a part of life a generation ago. To ease your own concerns about safety and security, investigate. Ask your child's principal or the school board questions about the concerns you have.

Dealing with Your Know-It-All Kid or Class Clown

It seems as if every classroom has one—a student who constantly makes comments, shows off, or cracks jokes in the middle of lessons. Class clowns may get the laughs, but there's nothing funny when it's your child who's disruptive.

A disruptive child can cause big problems for himself as well as classmates. A know-it-all can quickly alienate other children and the teacher. They can prevent other students from participating or learning the lesson and often miss opportunities to learn themselves. Class clowns, while providing levity to the classroom, disrupt lessons and make it difficult for the teacher to keep or regain control. Like know-it-alls, class clowns frequently prevent learning—their classmates' as well as their own.

Children are class clowns for a variety of reasons. Sometimes they are simply highly creative people who naturally love to entertain. Or they may thrive on excitement and when none is around, they create some with gags, practical jokes, or funny remarks. More often than not, though, they are using humor or disruptive behavior to distract others from an underlying problem.

Know-it-alls are not just gifted or bright children who eagerly participate in class, they are children who dominate the class, going out of their way to show off their knowledge, frequently answering questions before being called on. They openly take delight in pointing out the mistakes of others, including the teacher. Unlike class clowns, there's typically one reason a child is a know-it-all: they are insecure. The last thing a know-it-all wants is to appear dumb, so let your child know there are "smarter" ways to make friends than to show off in class.

Regardless of why a child is acting up or disrupting class, parents need to respond immediately. Waiting for the problem to go away on its own won't work. Waiting can also be harmful because disruptive children are often labeled as "trouble" and labels often perpetuate behavior. If you suspect your child is being disruptive in the classroom—or you've been told she is—the first thing you need to do is ask the teacher some questions. How frequent is the behavior? Is it all day? In a particular class? Is the behavior keeping my child from succeeding? Is it hurting his or her relationship with you or classmates? What have you tried so far to address the situation? You should also ask your child questions: What's your version of events? Why do you think you're behaving this way? Your child will probably not know why she is acting up, but opening lines of communication lets your child know you take her classroom conduct seriously and are willing to work together to improve things. It might also help you pinpoint the underlying cause for the behavior. Continue the conversation with your child by acknowledging that it's natural to like attention but that there is an appropriate place and time for getting it.

REASONS FOR DISRUPTIVE BEHAVIOR

*There are many reasons children might be disruptive in the class-
room. It's important to figure out the underlying problem and
address the issue and behavior quickly. Disruptive children might*

- *be ill or in physical pain;*

- *have ADD (Attention Deficit Disorder) or ADHD (Attention Deficit
  Hyperactivity Disorder);*

- *be gifted and bored;*

- *have Oppositional Defiance Disorder;*

- *be depressed;*

- *have an undiagnosed hearing or eyesight problem;*

- *be experiencing a problem with the teacher or a
  classmate and doesn't know what to do about it;*

- *lack impulse control;*

- *want attention.*

Next, you and your child should meet with the teacher and figure
out how to address the problem. A highly effective approach is a
daily report. For example, your child's teacher can send home a
note with smiley stickers or stars or comments about your child's
behavior that you sign and return. Set up a reward system. Let
your child work toward a desired toy or activity for improved
behavior. (This approach is known as behavior modification.) As a
parent, be sure to share any suggestions about approaches to try
or ones you already use effectively at home. What's done at home
and what's done at school should compliment each other.

Have your child come up with a signal you and the teacher can
use to tell him "enough is enough." For example, maybe the
teacher can turn down a pretend dial or tug an ear lobe.

Also, provide your child with an outlet for his energy. Sign him up
for theater classes where comedic talents are appreciated and

appropriate. Encourage your child to perform in the school talent show. Arrange for your know-it-all to help a younger student. (Just be sure you're present to make sure your child isn't dominating the younger one or being disrespectful.)

And finally, be your child's biggest cheerleader. Often times when there's a problem with classroom behavior, it can seem to children that's all anyone focuses on. Their teacher is frustrated. Other kids are resentful. The last thing your child needs is for you to be on his case all the time, too.

"Umm...er...umm" Fear of Giving an Oral Report

Your son steps off the bus looking pale and clutching a piece of paper. Is he in trouble at school or is the paper a notice there's strep throat going around? Neither, you discover as you gently pry the paper from his hand. Your son has to give an oral report in class.

Fear of public speaking is quite common. In some surveys, people rank the fear of public speaking higher than the fear of dying! The racing heart, the sweating, the queasy stomach—plenty of kids feel as if they're dying when they're standing in front of a group. But becoming a good public speaker (or at least one that doesn't throw up on friends in the front row) is something your child can do. You can help.

INSIDER TIP

Show-and-Tell (often called Sharing these days) is a time-honored tradition of kindergarten and first grade. It is also one way teachers prepare children for future oral reports. Letting children share a special object or event with their peers boosts young students' confidence by giving them a chance to speak in front of a group in a casual, non-threatening setting. Encourage your child to participate even if it is not required.

NOT SPEAKING AT ALL IN CLASS

Most people are at least somewhat uncomfortable about speaking in public. Some children, though, are extremely anxious about having to speak in front of the class—or have a difficult time speaking up in class at all. If your child is one of these children, she may have Social Anxiety Disorder. Children with this anxiety disorder are completely over-whelmed in social settings. It's more than just being shy; they may avoid eye contact or avoid classmates and teachers altogether. They may sweat, tremble, or become sick to their stomach when faced with having to speak to someone. The consequences are that your child may be a loner, or viewed by classmates as standoffish. Your child's education may even suffer if she is unwilling to ask for help.

But there's hope. In addition to seeking professional help or advice from your child's pediatrician or mental health professional, you can help your child deal with his extreme anxiety by (1) Praising and rewarding any small step of courage or positive change. For example, telling another child his name when asked or looking someone in the eye. (2) Helping your child brainstorm relaxation techniques that will work for him. For instance, if taking deep breaths doesn't work, perhaps counting to ten before speaking will help.

Another common reason a child doesn't speak up in class is depression. If your child used to participate in class and now seems to have mentally or emotionally dropped out of school, says things like, "I don't care," doesn't show interest in things he once enjoyed, or exhibits any other signs of depression, you need to have him evaluated by a professional right away.

First, explain to your child he will feel more confident if he is prepared. Help him come up with a manageable work schedule to research and write the report. Circle the project's due date on the calendar.

Next, help your child practice. Be a good audience by giving your child your full attention. If you must offer criticism, soften the blow with a few positive comments. For example, "I like the way you used a joke to open the report. Next time, how about using a louder voice so your classmates don't miss the great punch line."

If your child isn't keen on trying out the presentation in front of you right off the bat, he can rehearse in front of stuffed animals or action figures. Even a poster will work. Visualization can help, too. Tell your son to close his eyes and see himself standing in front of the class and delivering his speech perfectly.

On the day of the big report, offer to let your child run through his speech one more time. A great last-minute rehearsal can be a confidence boost. Remind your child that anticipating doing something you don't like is often worse than actually doing it. Tell him that when it's his turn to give his presentation he should take a deep breath, pick out a friendly face, and begin speaking. (Pretending you are speaking to only one person is a great way to de-wing those butterflies fluttering in your stomach.) Reminding your child everyone in his classroom is "in the same boat" and wants to see him succeed might also ease jitters. Finally, help your child put things into perspective. Ask him: "What's the worst that can happen?" and "How likely is it that the worst will happen?"

Fear of Using the School Bathroom

It's four o'clock and the bus has just pulled up outside. You can hear your son running into the house and down the hall. "I gotta go! It's an emerrrrrrgency!" You can't help but wonder— for the millionth time—Why won't the silly kid just use the bathroom at school?!

Fear of using a public bathroom or of using any bathroom when people are nearby is surprisingly common. The condition is called shy bladder, bashful bladder, shy kidneys, and even pee-phobia. The clinical term is paruresis and, though more common in boys, it can affect both sexes and children of all ages. According to the International Paruresis Association, seventeen million people struggle with this social phobia. No matter what you call it, dealing with the fear is a challenge. "Holding it in" all day long is not healthy and pretty darn uncomfortable. Kidney and bladder problems, urinary tract infections, as well as constipation can result if your child is unwilling or unable to use the bathroom at school.

There are many reasons your child could be uncomfortable using the bathroom during the school day. For example, bullies or other traumatic events in the restroom can cause bathroom anxiety. But many children are reluctant to use the school bathroom because of—no big surprise—privacy issues. ("Ew! The boys are right next door. They can hear me pee!" or "What if a girl accidentally walks in while I'm standing at the urinal?") Many newer schools have open entry bathrooms, an attempt to cut down on mischief. It's not likely you'll be able to convince your child's school to put doors on bathrooms; you should insist, however, that all stalls have doors and working locks for those doors.

For some kids, even having a private stall to use will not be enough. If your child has given the school bathroom issue some thought and is still unwilling or unable to go, ask his teacher if he can use the restroom at a separate time than the class. Consider that sometimes kindergartners and first graders are reluctant to

THOSE DARN AUTOMATIC FLUSHING TOILETS!

If your child is avoiding the bathroom at school because of the automatic toilets, try these suggestions. Is the unpredictability making your daughter nervous? Have her carry a Post It note with her to cover the red sensor button. Draping toilet paper over a motion sensor will also allow your child to flush when she's ready. If it's the loud sound of the toilet scaring your child, visiting bathrooms together can help your daughter overcome her fears. Show her how the toilet works and let her wave her hand in front of the sensor a few times to hear how loud the flush will be. (By the way, if the toilet doesn't flush, tell your child all she has to do is push the button under the sensor.)

use the school bathroom simply because it's unfamiliar, so give it a few weeks. If avoiding the school restroom continues to be a challenge, consider seeking professional help from a counselor who specializes in phobias.

Accidents at School

It's the stuff of nightmares—wetting your pants at school. How can you help when your child waited too long to use the bathroom and has had an accident? First, try not to make a big deal of it. Your child is already embarrassed. The less you fuss, the better. Second, don't scold your child. He didn't choose to lose control of his bladder or bowels. Third, reassure your child these things happen to just about everyone at some time or another and chances are good, few, if any, people probably noticed. Fourth, help your child come up with a good reply, just in case. "I left school early yesterday because I wasn't feeling well," which is true if your child had diarrhea.

Toileting accidents are common in young students. If you have a kindergartner or an older child who is playing "bathroom roulette" by avoiding the school restroom, consider discreetly packing a change of clothes in your child's backpack. Your child will feel more comfortable in his or her own clothes, and the school will not have to call you. Make sure to change the clothes each season so your child isn't stuck wearing shorts in the middle of winter.

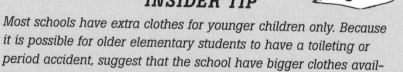

INSIDER TIP

Most schools have extra clothes for younger children only. Because it is possible for older elementary students to have a toileting or period accident, suggest that the school have bigger clothes available. Consider donating your child's outgrown clothes to the school for this purpose. Some child will be grateful!

GETTING A PERIOD AT SCHOOL

It doesn't matter if it's your first period, unexpected spotting, or a leak. Being caught off guard by a period at school can be mortifying to a young girl. But you can help your daughter.

- Tell her what to expect. While the typical age is somewhere between twelve and sixteen, girls as young as nine can experience menstruation. Don't let your daughter be caught off guard; talk to her about what she can expect as she moves into puberty. Also, be sure to explain what her first period might look like so she recognizes it when it happens. First periods are often light so your daughter might notice a brown stain in her underwear or a pink stain on toilet paper after she wipes.

- Encourage her to keep sanitary pads in her backpack. Because you never know when to expect your first period and because menstruation is frequently irregular in young girls, many girls carry sanitary pads or tampons in their backpacks. Brainstorm together some ways she could discreetly retrieve these items if needed. For example, girls could slip a pad in between the pages of a book and carry the book to the restroom. Slipping a tampon or a pad inside a long sleeve works too.

- Tell her where to go for help. Your daughter can go to the school nurse if she has a problem with her period, or to any female teacher for help. Explain that any female around will understand and do what she can to help. (Male teachers are sympathetic, too, of course, but your daughter will probably feel more comfortable with a woman.) If your daughter is too embarrassed to speak or worried about being overheard, tell her she can write a note and pass it to a teacher. Give her a few universal "code phrases" that will get her point across. For example, "I need to go to the nurse for a personal reason/girl stuff."

- Talk about cramps. They can be quite uncomfortable. Remind your daughter not to take any medicine from home to school or to borrow any from other students. If she needs to, your daughter should go to the nurse to lie down or have the nurse call home.

Cafeteria Conundrums

Your first grader comes bursting through the door, drops her backpack in the hallway and heads straight for the refrigerator without so much as a hello. "I'm staaarving," she tells you. Is it a growth spurt? Nope. She just didn't eat lunch. Again.

Not finishing lunch or not eating lunch at all is a surprisingly common problem for kids. It's also frustrating for parents because, short of going to school every day and feeding your child by hand, there's nothing you can do that will guarantee your child will eat. There are things you can do, however, to keep your child from turning into the Raider of the Last Tart every afternoon. Lunch problems are often a result of one of four things:

Your child is a victim of plain ol' bad timing.
Even a small school can have a difficult time getting all its students through the cafeteria in a reasonable amount of time. Unfortunately, this means some students must eat very early. Their internal clocks are not in sync with their school schedule and therefore they are simply not hungry when it's time to eat.

More than likely, there's nothing you can do about when your child is scheduled to eat at school. Insisting your child eat everything on her plate when she's not hungry is not a good idea; it can lead to unhealthy attitudes toward food. So if your child's lunchtime is a mere few hours after breakfast, pack a lighter lunch. A bit of protein, like string cheese or a hard-boiled egg, is easily managed and will ward off hunger. Fruit is also a good choice. If your child buys lunch, tell her it's okay to eat only one or two items and encourage her at least to drink her milk. If your child doesn't want to eat at all during the scheduled lunch time, see if her teacher will allow students to eat something from their lunch later in the day or will allow children to bring a snack from home to ease grumbling stomachs. Offering to bring in an after-

SCHOOL LUNCH NUTRITION

Jokes about "mystery meat" aside, Congress passed the National
School Lunch Program (NSLP) in 1946 as a way to ensure all school
children have access to healthy lunches. Under the program,
schools receive subsidies and donated commodities for providing
free or low-cost lunches to eligible students. The lunches must meet
certain dietary guidelines. More specifically, the lunches must provide one-third of the recommended daily allowance of protein,
vitamins A and C, iron, calcium, and calories. No more than 30 percent of those calories can be from fat and less than 10 percent can
be from saturated fat.

Because of the increase of type II diabetes, childhood obesity, high
cholesterol, and dozens of other health issues,
nutritionally balanced school lunches are
vital. Some school lunch programs are
falling short, though. Why? In
general, though the NSLP out-
lines what dietary needs must
be met, they do not dictate
what foods are served or how
they are prepared. The guidelines also do not have a fiber require-
ment and allow schools to offer other foods. These à la carte items
are often things like cookies, chips, and other high-sugar, high-fat,
high-sodium foods that tempt kids away from healthier choices.

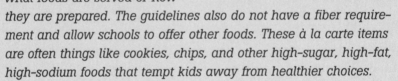

As a parent you can help improve the nutrition of school lunches
and the nutrition of your child:

• Be a good role model at home. Provide a wide variety of
  healthy snack options.

• Send in healthy snacks for birthdays, parties, or when it's your
  turn to provide class snack.

• Lobby for the removal of vending machines at school or for lim-
  iting their accessibility to students.

• Encourage your child's school to make more fresh fruit available.

continued

- *Limit the number of times you send in extra money for à la carte items to once a week. Also, make sure the school doesn't allow children to use their lunch cards to buy à la carte items.*

- *Speak up if your child's teacher is using food as a reward or a punishment in class.*

- *Eat lunch with your child at school occasionally.*

noon snack for the class (or arrange a rotating snack schedule for parents) might convince a teacher—if a classroom full of cranky kids doesn't seem to be doing the trick.

In addition to scheduling very early and late lunch times, schools frequently shorten the amount of time kids have to eat in order to squeeze everyone in. It's not unusual for students to have as little as twenty minutes for lunch, and this includes time to go through the lunch line and chit chat with friends! Your child may simply be running out of time to eat. You might try packing your child's lunch. In general, packers have a few extra minutes since they can sit down right away.

Your child is too stressed to eat. A chronic No Luncher may be anxious. Things such as having to sit at an assigned seat or to be silent throughout the meal, or even just going through the lunch line can be overwhelming for kids. Fears about dropping a tray or spilling food on their clothes or accidentally shooting milk out their nose can also put knots in kids' stomachs. Address your child's concerns and help her come up with a game plan. For example, ask her to consider what's the worst thing that could happen if she did drop her tray. Mostly likely, people would look up, giggle, and then quickly go back to eating. Talk about what your child could do next. For example, pick up the tray, ask a lunch volunteer to help, and get another lunch.

If your child is worried about going through the lunch line for the first time, ask her teacher to assign a buddy who can walk her through it. If assigned seating or other restrictions are the issue, try talking to the principal about a change. Kids need to relax and socialize at lunch. Chances are, if your child is anxious about the environment, other kids are feeling the same way.

Your child is not a lunch kind of kid. Some kids don't "do" lunch. Maybe they prefer to eat a huge breakfast or dinner. Maybe there's too much going on in their heads or lives to be interested in a midday meal. Maybe they just don't like lunch foods. There is no reason your child can't be a bit creative in her lunch choices. For example, pack your child a slice of cold pizza, a baggie of cereal with a thermos of milk, fruit-filled trail mix, or pretzels and peanut butter to dip them in. Often, several finger foods (such as half a sandwich or a handful of cheese cubes) are more appealing to a child who doesn't have the appetite for a conventional meal but does have a conscientious parent.

Your child is a picky eater. Living with an I'm-not-eating-that-and-you-can't-make-me kid can be a real pain in the lunchbox. Since you probably don't have the time (or desire) to go to school and monitor your child's lunch habits every day, you'll have to resort to other tactics. Allowing a finicky eater to help you pack her lunch or pick out the lunchbox or food containers can help by giving your child a sense of control. Bringing your child with you to the grocery store and having her choose a few foods for school lunches is another good way to ease food battles. Don't give up good nutrition, though. It's important to offer a variety of healthy foods. And even if your child isn't eating the bananas you packed, keep sending them. Eventually, she may give them a taste.

Chapter 4

Making The Grade : Academic Issues

It's a Friday afternoon and your son looks a little pale as he grips the large envelope that holds his report card. "All right, buddy. Hand it over," you say. "It can't be all that bad."

While your son watches anxiously, you read over the report card. No. It's not all that bad. (The C in math is now a B.) But it's not all that great either. Apparently, the teacher still feels that your son isn't working to his full potential.

Test anxiety. Cheating. Failing a test or a grade. Learning disabilities. Dealing with a gifted child, an underachiever, or a gifted underachiever. Or dealing with one child who gets straight A's and another who is a solid C student. Wouldn't it be great if you could just go to the store and pick up some study guides on how to help your child make the grade at school?

Test Anxiety

You quizzed your daughter for the test every night for two weeks. She was confident and prepared. (After all that quizzing, *you* could've aced the test.) And now, it's the moment of truth—the day the test is returned. Your daughter hands you her paper. It's not good. Unless that big, red D at the top stands for *dandy*, your daughter might have test anxiety.

Sometimes the heightened anxiety felt before or during an exam prevents students from performing as well as they can. Other times, it simply wreaks havoc on his nerves. Sweating, shaking hands, a racing heart, a stomachache, nail biting, and insomnia in the days before an exam are just a few of the signs of test anxiety. Whether your child is a bit jittery or a big bundle of nerves, there are things you can do to help.

First, help your child prepare. Cramming for a test is seldom a good idea. As soon as your child finds out about an exam, help her come up with a study schedule. Because learning in bits and pieces will aid in retention, break up material into smaller, more

HOW LONG TO STUDY?

How long your child should study is largely based on her age. In general, the younger the child, the shorter the amount of time she can study effectively. (Developmentally, younger children have shorter attention spans than older children.) Every child's concentration level is different and circumstances may warrant a higher study load on occasion, but according to the National Parent-Teacher Organization, children in kindergarten, first, or second grade should study no longer than fifteen to twenty minutes a day. Children in third through sixth grade should study no longer than thirty to sixty minutes. Insisting your child study anything longer than these times will not improve retention and only frustrate everyone involved.

INSIDER TIP

Don't have an all-or-nothing attitude and don't allow your child to stress too much over one test. A test is only a test. Nothing horrible will happen if your child does poorly; she can still become a productive member of society despite the fact she misspelled "anonymous" on a spelling test in fourth grade. The same goes for a bad report card or even a rotten school year. Help make your point with your child by asking if she'd throw away all of her toys if just one or two broke. Chances are she wouldn't—and you probably wouldn't do that, either!

manageable chunks. If your child is not overly sensitive to deadlines, circle the test date on a calendar, (for some kids, circling a date only heightens the anxiety). If you don't have time set aside for homework each day already, have your child decide when study time should be each day. Encourage your child to take into consideration his natural body rhythm. For example, some children like to get a snack and unwind for a bit after school. Their minds are ready to work again after dinner. Other children find it easier to come straight home and do homework or study while their brains are still in "school mode." Don't allow study time to be too late, though. Sitting down to review for a test right after a big meal or before bed isn't a good idea because children are apt to be too tired to retain information well.

LEARNING STYLES

Knowing your child's particular learning style can make helping him or her with schoolwork much less frustrating for everyone and more productive for your child. There are a variety of learning styles, but most people fall into one of three main categories.

*Your child is an **auditory learner** if he learns best when he talks about lessons or hears material read out loud. Auditory learners are good at memory games and music and remember details they've heard. To help your auditory learner study, have him make up rhymes or recite information to a beat or a familiar tune. You can help by discussing what he's studying or having him explain how to work out a problem or spell a word over and over.*

*Your child is a **visual learner** if he does better when he can see or visualize information. Visual learners respond well to material written on blackboards or posters and remember details they've seen. You can help your visual learner by encouraging him to make flash cards or an outline of the material he needs to review. Or give your child a highlighter or colored markers to use on his notes.*

*Your child is a **kinesthetic learner** if he learns best by doing. These kinds of children love to act out problems, handle things, and take apart things to see how they work. They remember details they've experienced. To help your kinesthetic learner, provide plenty of manipulatives (such as pennies, blocks, toy cars, etc.) to play around with or have him act out a problem.*

If you're not sure which style your child is, try several approaches. Even though children tend to learn better from one or two approaches, it doesn't mean they won't benefit from trying something different. This is why teachers go over new material in a variety of ways. Students respond to different things at different times. And finally, there's one last important thing to keep in mind—parents and children often have different learning styles. Don't fall into the trap of thinking that just because you like to study one way means your child should study that way too. Avoid tears of frustration (yours and your child's) by backing off and letting your child decide how he wants to study.

INSIDER TIP

In many states, parents can refuse to allow their children to participate in proficiency testing. But, unless your child is terribly distraught about taking the tests or for some reason you're deeply concerned the test wouldn't adequately measure your child's abilities, it's generally best to let your child be tested. Many children experience stress because of the change of routine and not because of the test itself. Whether or not your child participates, his routine will be affected. Besides, evaluations are a part of life and taking proficiency tests is good practice for things down the road like college entrance exams, drivers' tests, and civil service exams.

When study time rolls around, remind your child to hit the books but don't nag. You're not the one taking a test, your child is! She should be responsible for preparing. Besides, pushing your child to study can backfire. Your child might become so anxious that she can't study effectively or become so fed up that she declares her independence by refusing to study at all. Your job during study time is to be available. If your child asks for help, offer to quiz her, but don't take over any part of preparation your child can do. For example, you can give spelling words or listen to your child recite the multiplication tables but *don't* rewrite notes or go through a textbook searching for an answer. If your child becomes frustrated or teary, suggest that she stop for a while or even for the day. When children are emotional, reason and learning slow way down. This goes for parents, too. If you feel yourself becoming anxious or frustrated, it's a sign you're too involved. Move away and let your child study alone.

On the day of the test, try not to discuss the test at great length. Suggest to your child that she doesn't talk about the test with her friends at school, either. Talking about an impending test will only raise anxiety levels. Some children feel better if they read through the material or go over their notes "one more time." This is fine, but discourage cramming. Suggest to your child that she try some relaxation techniques (see Chapter 3) during the exam.

WHAT ABOUT PROFICIENCY TESTS?

Proficiency tests have been hotly debated recently. Many parents and educators criticize these standardized tests for, among other things, being biased against certain socio-economic groups, not adequately measuring student performance, and putting children and teachers under undue stress. There is also debate over how test results should be used. Typically given over the course of a week, proficiency tests are used to determine a child's progress and whether or not teachers are meeting certain statewide curriculum standards. The results are also frequently used to determine how students compare to other students nationwide or how a school district compares to another within the state. They can, in some cases, determine which schools receive monetary aid. Many states also use test results to determine whether or not a child is promoted to the next grade, or placed in remedial or gifted classes or summer school. Test results may even affect whether or not an older child receives a diploma. When used this way, proficiency tests are considered "high-stakes testing." Because of these high-stakes issues and because they disrupt the school routine, proficiency tests can cause anxiety in even the most laid-back kids.

Love 'em or hate 'em, proficiency tests are a part of school life. In the last few years, there's been a push to make taking these tests less stressful for students. For example, some schools are doing things such as bringing in yoga instructors or inviting parents to write encouraging notes that kids can read before a test. As a parent, you can help support your child during proficiency test time by making sure he is well rested and eats a nutritious breakfast before the tests. You can also provide a snack and water bottle if your child is allowed to take them and simply encourage him or her to do his or her best. The best thing you can do for your child is to relax yourself! If you are calm about proficiency tests, your child will be too.

Cheating

Complete the following: Cheating is . . .

A. Copying answers off someone
else's test.

B. Having someone else do your homework or doing someone else's work.

C. Looking at a test or its answer key ahead of time.

D. All of the above and more.

E. Just a minute, I've gotta consult my crib notes.

Cheating is so common that it's safe to say most kids will cheat in
some way, shape, or form at least once while in school. Of course,
just because everyone seems to be doing it doesn't make it right.

Children cheat for a variety of reasons. Younger students (in kindergarten and first grade) sometimes cheat because they simply aren't
developmentally old enough to understand that it is wrong. They
need an answer. Someone else has it. Why not share? (Or take it?)
Younger children also tend to be more impulsive than older students and not able to fully appreciate or foresee the consequences
of cheating. Older students can foresee the consequences but may
not care or decide what they need or want now is more important.
Sometimes they cheat because they're curious about what it's like
to break the rules or want to see what they can get away with.
Sometimes it's because they're lazy or don't know how to properly
study. Other times it's because they are struggling with the work
and are afraid to speak up or that they feel pressure (from parents
or themselves) to perform well in school. Many students, both
young and old, cheat just because the opportunity to do so comes
up. (It's like Sir Edmund Hillary saying he climbed Mt. Everest,
"Because it's there.")

Can You "Cheat Proof" Your Child?

First of all, talk to your child and define cheating. You and your
child should read over your school's policy about cheating
together so you and your child know what is expected at school.

Be clear about what you consider cheating and what you expect, as well. Let your child know you will not tolerate any cheating, whether it is in school, at home, or on the sports field.

Second, discuss the serious consequences of cheating. Most children aren't developmentally able to appreciate the old "you're only cheating yourself" line, but they do understand results. Warn your child that getting caught may mean getting a zero on a test, failing a class or the semester, being expelled, grounded, or worse— being labeled untrustworthy by your peers. In addition to talking to your child about cheating and its consequences, be a good role model. Don't keep mum when the cashier hands you back extra change. Don't count your dog as a dependent on your tax return. And don't peek at the answers while playing Trivial Pursuit.

Third, be mindful about putting undue pressure on your child. Place emphasis on getting a good education, not perfect grades.

PLAGIARISM

Plagiarism—copying something another person has written and pretending it's your own—is a form of cheating. Young children sometimes plagiarize because they are unaware it's wrong. And even if they are aware that using someone's words or ideas is wrong, the Internet has made cheating easy and tempting. Because so much is out there and easily accessible, some students figure "No one will ever know I copied!" (Why it seldom occurs to them that parents and teachers might be suspicious when they use a word such as antidisestablishmentarianism is one of life's mysteries!)

You can help your child avoid plagiarism by reading over his work, asking him to explain the material to you (which will demonstrate whether or not he has internalized the material or is simply spitting it out by rote), and helping your child properly format quotes and other material that needs to be cited.

WHAT COUNTS AS CHEATING?

Part of the problem with cheating and explaining it to children is the "gray area." While there are things generally accepted as cheating (like looking at another student's paper), there are many other actions that aren't so clear-cut. For example, some kids, parents, and teachers see nothing wrong with kids checking homework answers with each other; others do.

So what is cheating? Simply put, cheating is deliberately misleading or deceiving someone or acting dishonestly. These concepts may be too abstract for your child, especially if he is very young. When explaining cheating, use age-appropriate language. For instance, a kindergartner or first or second grader will understand "lying" or "taking something that isn't yours." An older child may understand the idea of "breaking the rules to get ahead." Give your child concrete examples. You can even play a game where you take turns coming up with scenarios and asking each other "Is this cheating?" Here are just a few examples of behavior that is universally viewed as cheating:

- *looking at or copying another person's paper or homework with or without their permission*
- *letting someone else look at or copy your work*
- *doing someone else's work for them or letting them do yours*
- *looking at an answer key before or during a test*
- *changing an answer (your own or another student's) while grading a paper or not marking an answer that's incorrect*
- *looking at unapproved notes during an exam or looking up an answer in a textbook without permission*
- *discussing test questions before you or a friend has taken the test*
- *plagiarizing*
- *breaking the rules of a game in order to affect the outcome*
- *lying to someone in order to affect the outcome of a game*

Tell your child you only want her to do her best. Overemphasizing or paying for high marks can cause some kids to resort to cheating, as can a child's own perfectionism.

If your child is caught cheating, be patient. The first thing many children do is deny the cheating. Explain why you and her teacher are suspicious. If you have to, show your child the evidence (such as papers with identical answers). Don't back down. A child who gets away with cheating once is likely to try to get away with it again.

Next, dig deeper. Once your child confesses—or even if she doesn't—try to find out why she cheated and respond appropriately. The occasional cheating offence, while serious, is nothing to panic about. Deal with it and then drop it. Frequent cheating, however, is often a symptom of a bigger problem. For example, if your daughter continually cheats on her math tests, it may be time to hire a tutor. If it's not a matter of understanding the material, perhaps the cheating is a cry for attention.

And finally, follow through. No matter how convincing her reasons or how remorseful she is, let your child experience the consequences of cheating. Perhaps a big, fat zero on a test that counts for half her grade or having to stay in from recess will make her think twice about cheating next time.

Failing or Falling Behind

There's a famous story about how Thomas Edison, when asked about his nearly 10,000 failed attempts, said, "I didn't fail. I just found 9,999 ways *not* to invent the light bulb." Failure may only be feedback, but when it's your son who's finding 9,999 ways *not* to pass science, it doesn't seem so simple.

Kids fail or fall behind in school for a variety of reasons: they lack motivation, perseverance, or good time management skills; they're so afraid of failing they procrastinate; they have an undiagnosed learning disability or hearing or eyesight problem; or they have a hard time concentrating or are struggling with problems outside of school that are distracting them or taking up a lot of energy. Gifted children sometimes fail because they are bored and tune out. Sometimes, kids are struggling with a particular subject and are afraid or embarrassed to ask for help.

Getting to the root of the problem is crucial. If your child is falling behind, don't wait, hoping your child will suddenly catch on and catch up, because it won't happen. A child who is falling behind needs help; otherwise the gap between her and her classmates will only get wider. On top of that, a child who is failing is vulnerable to low self esteem, depression, and ridicule from other students.

If your child is falling behind or failing a class, contact the teacher and ask the following questions:

How far behind is my child? This will help give you the scope of the problem. For example, if your child is only somewhat behind his classmates, a few extra after-school sessions with the teacher may be all it takes to get him back on track. If, however, your child is way behind, it may be time to find a tutor. Hopefully your child's teacher has contacted you at the first sign of trouble.

When did you notice my child was beginning to slip? Asking this may help shed light on what is causing the slip in grades or motivation.

What do you think is causing the trouble? Teachers are experts in child development and spend all day with your child. They often have great insight as to why a student is falling behind or failing a subject.

What have you tried in the classroom? You may have another suggestion that will work better.

What can I do to help at home? This question lets your child's teacher know that you are willing to support her and

HOW TO FIND A TUTOR

Call your child's school or ask around. Neighbors, friends, or co-workers may know the name of someone. A tutoring or educational service may advertise in local newspapers. Nearby colleges or local high schools may have students who are quite capable and willing to help younger students. Many of them are also looking for ways to earn community service hours or to beef up their college applications. Once you've found a name or two, be sure to interview the prospective tutors.

Consider your child's personality and needs when considering candidates.

your child. More importantly, it gives you some practical ideas to use.

Is there anything else I should be aware of? Again, teachers are around your child all day. Perhaps there are other things happening in the classroom that could be clues to your child's struggle. For example, maybe your child is being teased about being smart. Even if nothing rings a bell right off the bat, just asking this question may lead your child's teacher to be more in tune to what's going on with your child.

You should also approach your child with similar questions:

What's happening? A child may know right away why she is struggling. ("I don't get fractions at all!" or "I can't see the chalkboard very well!") Your child may have a completely different story to tell about what is happening at school. For example, maybe there are many other kids who are falling behind or failing. This might indicate that there is a problem with the way the teacher is presenting the materials.

What can your teacher and I do to help you? This question shows your child that you and the teacher are not "out to get" her. You want to help. Many children have surprisingly good and

COMFORTING A CHILD WHO'S FAILED

It's never easy to watch your child fail, especially if you know he's worked hard on a project or really studied for a test. And if your child didn't prepare the way he should have, it's tempting to say "Tough noogies." But this is not what your child needs to hear. Along with a hug (and maybe some warm chocolate chip cookies), try one of these phrases:

- *"I love you no matter what."* Your child needs to know your love is unconditional, not based on school performance.

- *"You'll do better next time."* This statement shows you have faith in your child's abilities.

- *"I failed a test, too."* Telling your child about a time you failed helps him see no one is perfect and that it's possible to overcome a mistake.

- *"What do you think went wrong? What do you think you'd do differently next time?"* These questions help your child take responsibility for his actions—or lack of action if that's the case.

- *"What's the plan for next time?"* Get your child thinking about what he can do to prevent another F on a test. Have him get specific. For example, instead of saying "I'll study longer," encourage him to commit, "I'll study every day for fifteen minutes."

- *"How can I help?"* This shows you're willing to support your child.

creative ideas about how to improve their skills!

After collecting details and identifying the problem (or at the very least, ruling out a few things) schedule a conference with your child and her teacher. As a team, decide on the best course of action. For example, if your child has poor management skills, she might benefit from a daily assignment or reminder sheet. If it's a family situation interfering with schoolwork, she might benefit from visiting with the school counselor. The important thing is to follow through and follow up. Continue to monitor her progress and occasionally check in with the teacher and your child.

Learning Disabilities

There are a variety of cognitive, neurological, or psychological disorders that can interfere with a person's ability to learn. They have nothing to do with a child's intelligence; most learning disabled people have an average or above average IQ. Learning disabilities affect both boys and girls equally, often run in families, and sometimes go undetected by parents and teachers for years. Early identification is important; it can make a huge difference in preserving children's self esteem and education.

The four most common learning disabilities are dyslexia (difficulties with language-based skills such as reading, spelling, grammar), dyscalculia (difficulties with numbers or with grasping mathematical concepts), dysgraphia (difficulties with handwriting, forming letters), and auditory and visual processing disabilities (difficulties with understanding and processing auditory or visual information even though vision and hearing are normal).

There are many, many signs a child may have a learning disability. It's important to note, though, all kids show one or more of these signs at some point; it doesn't mean they have a disability. Just a few of the more common red flags to watch for include being slow to make letter/sound connections, confusing basic sight words, consistently inverting or transposing letters when reading or writing, poor handwriting or awkward pencil grip, slow recall of facts or relying heavily on memorization, trouble learning about time or inability to keep numbers in columns when doing math, difficulty copying material from board, difficulty in concentrating or completing work on time, impulsiveness, general clumsiness, and a tendency to misinterpret behavior of peers or adults.

If your child is showing several signs or if you have concerns about something not on the list, ask the school's counselor or psychologist about having a full evaluation done. And be prepared. Even when the school agrees there is cause for concern, the evaluation process can be long and frustrating. In order to provide your child with services, he must meet numerous, state-determined criteria. Some parents opt to have their child tested independently, which can be expensive, and may or may not be covered by insurance. It can, however, speed up the process of getting your child the help she needs. It may also be the only option if your child's school doesn't believe there is a cause for concern. It's not uncommon for a teacher to be unfamiliar with the signs of learning disabilities or for the signs of the disability to be so subtle that the problem is overlooked or downplayed. Parents' instincts telling them there's something not quite right is sometimes the driving force behind a child being evaluated. If you're concerned your child has a learning disability but the school isn't, don't back down. Be your child's advocate. Children with learning disabilities can be highly successful in school if their unique learning needs are addressed.

Motivating an Underachiever

It's report card day and your child hands you the envelope. Hoping for the best (but prepared for the worst), you open the envelope and do a quick scan. It's a sea of C's. You wouldn't be upset if the grades truly reflected your child's ability, but they don't. You know your child is capable of so much more. And so does she, judging by the sheepish look on her face!

If your child is not reaching his potential, there are things you can do to encourage your child to do his best in school.

Have high but realistic expectations. If you treat your child as if she is capable of doing well, she will. Be mindful, though, of putting undue pressure on your child. It might not be reasonable to expect an A from your child; maybe a C is the best she can do.

Let the child decide on goals . . . Your child will be more likely to work toward goals that she has set herself.

. . . but be ready to step in if her goals are too low. Sometimes, children are so afraid of failing that they will settle for hilltops instead of mountain summits. If your child is setting her sights too low, offer a deal. Tell her she can choose a goal but she must also work toward a goal you've set. Another approach is to challenge her to "surprise herself" and go just a bit further. The word surprise has a positive connotation. Most people like to feel they've gone an extra mile or given 110 percent.

Provide opportunities for success. Success breeds success. This is why some teachers begin the school year with work most children will find fairly easy. Providing an opportunity for success may be as simple as picking out a book you know your child will be able to read with little assistance.

Praise and reward. Let your child know when she's done well! Surprise her every once in awhile with a treat to show her hard work pays off. Also, make sure you're rewarding her for good effort and not only for good results.

Build on your child's strengths. Play up your child's strong points. For example, if your daughter knows a lot about dinosaurs, encourage her to write or read stories about them.

Provide your child with the tools necessary for success. For example, if your child is trying to improve her reading skills, support her efforts by buying her a new reading light she can use at bedtime.

Show your child how what she's learning is useful. Take any opportunity to point out how what your child is learning is meaningful *in her life*. For instance, your daughter might not care about math, but knowing fractions will help her fairly divide a pizza on Friday night.

Don't intentionally or unintentionally set up competition between siblings. Each child is uniquely talented. Some things may come easier for one child than another. Let each of your children know they are valued for who they are and what they are.

Being Held Back

Repeating a grade was more common a generation or two ago than it is today. Because numerous studies indicate holding a child back can put her at greater risk for poor self esteem, failing, and even dropping out of school, schools are extremely reluctant to recommend this course of action. That said, there are times when holding your child back may be the best thing. It's heartbreaking to hear your child may benefit from repeating a grade, but teachers do not recommend retention lightly. If your child's teacher is telling you that you might want to consider the option, listen. Some students need an extra year to grow and mature emotionally or to practice skills, or have missed too much school due to illness or some other reason to be confidently promoted.

There's a lot of debate about whether or not retention works. Experts generally agree, however, that the earlier, the better. A

INSIDER TIP

Some school districts are experimenting with special, transitional classes for kids who have completed kindergarten but aren't quite ready for first grade. These classrooms are sometimes called K–1s or Transitional first.

younger child (one in third grade or below) is likely to have an easier time—emotionally and academically—than an older child who is held back. It is also generally accepted that it is not enough to simply repeat a grade; the following year must be different somehow (for example, a different teacher, different teaching approach, even a different school.) If your child has failed a grade because of some issue and that issue is not addressed, repeating the grade won't be beneficial. Weigh the pros and cons carefully.

Because it can be difficult to determine if a child should be held back and the issue is often an emotionally charged one for parents, the majority of schools have an assessment plan that frequently includes a formal evaluation instrument such as the Lights Retention Scale. Using these types of scales, a child receives points for having a late summer birthday or having had academic intervention or an identified learning disability and so forth. The points are then added and scored.

In addition to a formal evaluation, the process will also likely include meetings between parents, teachers, and other appropriate school personnel, where your child's teacher will share her specific concerns and reasons for recommending retention. This is your opportunity to share your feelings as well. You know your

The **PROS** of holding your child back a grade include extra time to grow emotionally and master necessary skills. Getting a "fresh start" in a new classroom or with a new teacher may make the child happier and less stressed out.

The **CONS** of holding your child back a grade include the reality that it can be very traumatic to a child. There is often a stigma to being held back, and it can be difficult for a child not to progress with friends. Your child won't be with children his own age, which may become a problem down the road in junior high and high school when kids develop physically and socially. Retention won't magically fix any problems that haven't been addressed, and the success of retention can't be predicted.

child better than the school does, so follow your instincts. If your child's school is telling you your child needs to be held back—or promoted—and you object, be prepared to battle. Do your homework. Be sure to clearly document the reasons you feel the way you do. This can mean bringing in samples of your child's work or having your child evaluated by an outside expert.

Gifted Children

Your third grader comes home sullen. You try everything you can think of to get him to talk, but it's not until bedtime that he opens up. "I don't want to go to school anymore!" he says. "All my classmates call me Genius Boy!" You try to reassure him there's nothing wrong with being smart, but he wants no part of it. Anything that makes you different from your peers when you're nine is tough.

Being a parent of an academically gifted child is often tough, too. One of the biggest tasks for parents of a gifted child is keeping their child challenged. Parents shouldn't rely on schools to do this. Sometimes, teachers are intimidated by or don't like or don't know how to deal with exceptionally bright children. Other times, teachers simply don't have the time or resources to work with the one or two gifted students in their classroom. Or they mistakenly believe a gifted student will thrive on his or her own.

INSIDER TIP

As a parent, it is up to you to decide whether or not to share your child's IQ or test scores with your child. Many parents of gifted children do not because the information can be a burden. Some children may feel pressure to always excel. Others may use it as an excuse not to try. ("I'm already smart enough.") Still, other children may use it when they get backed into a corner or want to feel superior. ("I'm smarter than you are!") When deciding what to tell your child, ask yourself, "How will it benefit my child to know her IQ score?"

PASS GO AND COLLECT YOUR REPORT CARD—SKIPPING A GRADE

Like repeating a grade, skipping a grade is another hot button issue for parents. On the surface, moving up a grade, also known as acceleration, seems like a wonderful idea for a gifted child. And indeed, there are gifted children who benefit tremendously from being placed with children who are their intellectual peers. But, like holding your child back, allowing your child to skip a grade requires careful consideration. It's important everyone involved— parents, teachers, child—are all in agreement. Experts also agree the final vote about whether to skip a grade or not should be your child's. Pushing a child into skipping a grade is never a good idea.

*The **PROS** of acceleration include the fact that your child will be with his intellectual peers and may find the new environment stimulating, which may lead to a new enthusiasm for school and learning. Many gifted children are already more comfortable with older children and so the transition is usually smooth. Some studies show that highly gifted students are happier when they are allowed to move ahead.*

*The **CONS** of acceleration include taking your child away from her social peers. She may be physically smaller than classmates, which may cause her to be picked on or cause problems later on when classmates begin to go through puberty and she doesn't. It's also possible that there will be gaps in learning or skills she missed that her classmates already have, and some students may struggle with not being at the "top of the class" anymore.*

It is important to challenge your gifted child. A gifted child who is not supported may become disruptive in the classroom and—even worse—become lazy or lose interest in school altogether. If your child has been identified as gifted, there are things you can do to help him reach his potential.

Be an advocate for your child. Getting to know your child's teacher is especially important when your child has special educational needs. Volunteer for the classroom or, at the very least,

be in regular contact with your child's teacher so if there's a concern, the lines of communication are already open. If your child's teacher is not supporting your child in the way you'd like, speak up. For example, it's not unusual for teachers to simply give gifted children *more* work instead of advanced work. Point out that your gifted child already knows how to do the work his classmates are doing; he doesn't need more practice, he needs *different* work. Another common occurrence is a teacher who requires students to make up work they missed while pulled out of the classroom for a gifted education class. Children should be required to make up only what is necessary, like a test. Otherwise, a gifted child may decide the extra work is punishment for being smart.

Making the teacher aware of any teaching or discipline techniques you've found that work with your child is a good idea, too. Maybe you've found that your child likes to read when he's stressed out or you know your child doesn't like to be praised in front of his peers. These types of insights are helpful to a teacher.

Help your child identify and expand on her talents. Gifted children often have a variety of interests. Support them any way you can. This may mean finding a piano teacher, a chess club, or an art institute that offers children's classes or a local author who's willing to mentor a young writer. It may also mean buying a telescope, going to the library each week to borrow books and videos, or relaxing about the mess when your dining room table is covered with a science experiment.

A DEFINITION OF GIFTED

"Gifted" is one of those words that gets thrown around too casually, a label that is frequently overused by parents and teachers. Every parent wants to believe his child is gifted. But while every child is special and has unique gifts, some children have exceptional talents that need to be addressed. In short, a gifted child is one who shows exceptionally high levels of performance or is capable of exceptionally high levels of performance compared to other children of her age, experience, or environment. Gifted children may exhibit superior talent in cognitive abilities, creative thinking skills, leadership capabilities, artistic areas such as visual or performing arts, or in one or more specific academic subjects (such as math or language arts). They may have talents in several of these areas or even all of them, with abilities so beyond their peers that they require specialized education.

Chances are your community has some great summer camps that would interest and challenge your gifted child as well. Check with your child's school, gifted education teacher, or your state's gifted education association for more information.

Make sure your child spends time with other gifted children. Gifted kids know they are different. Sometimes, they feel confused, frustrated, or even ashamed they are not like their classmates. Just like everyone else, gifted kids need to feel as if they belong and that who they are is okay, so make sure they have opportunities to be with their intellectual peers.

Respect your child's difference but don't coddle him. Your child may have the IQ of a genius, but he is still a child. Read to him, kiss him, spoil him, and make him clean up his room on Saturdays. Don't let his giftedness be an excuse to get away with poor behavior. And don't let being gifted be the only thing he identifies himself by. It is just one of many things that makes him special.

SOME SIGNS OF GIFTEDNESS

You know your child is very bright . . . but gifted? Sometimes a child's academic talents are obvious. Other times a child's giftedness goes unnoticed because of behavioral problems, underachievement, or poor test-taking skills. Though no two gifted children are the same, many exhibit

- *a tendency to reach developmental milestones early (for example, rolling over, walking, and talking);*
- *an advanced vocabulary and/or memory;*
- *a wide variety of interests;*
- *a high level of concentration that allows them to work on a project for long periods of time;*
- *strong leadership skills;*
- *an excellent (or advanced) sense of humor;*
- *a vivid imagination;*
- *the ability to think abstractly;*
- *a preference to be with older children or adults.*

Gifted children may also be highly sensitive, highly active, or exhibit perfectionism or behavioral problems.

Your Special-Needs Child

One of the most important jobs of parenthood is being an advocate for your child. This is especially true if you have a child who has special needs.

If your child was born with a disability or his acquired disability is severe, chances are you've been around the bases a few times. Starting school can be a whole new ballgame, though. It is understandably overwhelming if your child has just been identified as having (or is suspected of having) special needs.

The Individuals with Disabilities Education Act (IDEA) is a federal law that requires all states to provide a free, appropriate education to children regardless of the severity of their disabilities. The two major components of this education are the Least Restrictive Environment (LRE) and an Individualized Education Plan (IEP). The Least Restrictive Environment means modifications must be made to the classroom or learning space for a child with special needs. An Individualized Education Plan is a detailed, written plan that addresses how the educational needs of a child will be met.

If your child has special needs, his or her IEP will be discussed and written up in what's called an IEP meeting. As a parent, you will receive written notice about when and where your child's IEP meeting will take place. It should be done when it is convenient for you as your attendance is vital. Other people who may be present include your child's teacher, a school district representative who will oversee the provided services, any appropriate service providers (such as a speech therapist, physical or occupational therapist, classroom aide), the person who evaluated your child or someone who can interpret the results of the evaluation, and, if appropriate, your child. Sometimes the principal will attend, as well. You may also request an interpreter if you need one.

At the meeting, the group will discuss and go over the results of any recent evaluations, talk about your child's strengths and weaknesses, determine specific, educational goals for your child, and write the IEP, which you will be asked to sign. All IEPs should include the following information: a statement identifying a child's disability, a statement of the child's current level of performance, long- and short-term educational goals, the procedure for how a child's progress toward those goals will be evaluated, a list of services or support

Special needs include mental disabilities, visual or hearing impairments, speech or communication delays or impairments, orthopedic impairments, severe emotional disturbances, neurological disorders such as autism, traumatic brain injuries, specific learning disabilities, and other health issues such as chronic illness or ADD/ADHD.

STOP

being made available to the child, the dates (and times, if appropriate) of when these services will take place, and the modifications, if any, that will be made to the classroom.

It may be very overwhelming to attend an IEP meeting, especially if the process is new to you. Information is buzzing around you like mosquitoes on a hot summer night. But as qualified as everyone in the room is, you're the number one expert when it comes to your child. At the meeting, listen carefully to what's being said, take notes, ask questions if you don't understand something, offer

WHAT IF YOUR CHILD IS SUSPECTED OF HAVING SPECIAL NEEDS?

If your child is suspected of having a special need, the first thing that will happen is you will receive a letter outlining the school's concerns and asking for your permission to test or evaluate your child. It's important to note that schools cannot evaluate a child without a parent's written permission. Read over the letter carefully and make sure you understand it. If you are confused about anything at all, call the person whose name is on the letter and ask questions. It can be distressing to find out your child is suspected of having a disability or developmental delay. If you have to, take a few days to let the information sink in and your emotions settle down.

After you have signed the permission form, the school will then evaluate your child. It is a good idea to warn your child he is going to be evaluated. Do this matter-of-factly, careful not to use the word "test" which might cause your child to panic. (He can't, after all, study for it.) Make sure to explain to your child he has done nothing wrong. Try saying something along the lines of "The school wants to find out what you already know and what you might need to work on." If you know the details, such as when, where, and how the evaluation will take place, share them with your child.

Within thirty days of testing, your child's eligibility for services will be decided. If after the evaluation it is found your child qualifies for services, you will be notified and an IEP meeting will be set up.

suggestions, and share information about your child. Feel free to argue a point. And don't sign the IEP until you're comfortable with it. A few things you might want to make sure are addressed to your satisfaction are Will there be an aide? What are the teacher's and aide's qualifications or experience in working with my child's particular disability? If the teacher or aide is absent, will the substitute be qualified? What modifications will be made in the room? How many kids will be in my child's class? How many of them, if any, also have special needs? What information, if any, will my child's classmates and their parents be given? How will my child's classmates' (and other parents') concerns be addressed? How will testing and grades be handled? How will I be notified of changes or problems?

What About Siblings?

It's Saturday afternoon and the whole family is making its way through the crowd at the big science fair. To your delight, you spot a big, blue ribbon by your older, gifted child's project. Your younger child's project doesn't even get an honorable mention ribbon. Your oldest is beaming. Your youngest is sullen.

As most parents quickly discover, children who come from the same parents and grow up in the same house with the same opportunities can be remarkably different from each other. Children naturally have different skills and talents, but when one of your children is gifted or has special needs and his siblings are or do not, it can be a real balancing act to meet everyone's emotional needs. Siblings, especially when they are close in age or the same gender, tend to be very competitive. There are ways, though, to help children with varying degrees of talent feel secure.

First of all, don't assume there is or isn't a problem. Just because your child doesn't seem to be too phased by her sibling's straight-A report card or science fair blue ribbon, doesn't mean she isn't bothered. When the two of you have a private moment, bring the subject up casually. Say something like, "So, how do you feel about your report card?" Take your child's lead. Don't look for trouble, though, by insisting your child "must be" upset or jealous of your other child's success. Your child may be perfectly comfortable with her own abilities. It's also important to note that some children may respond to a sibling's success by acting out or becoming the family or class clown.

Spend time alone with each child. Giving children an opportunity to have the spotlight all to themselves can make having to share it later on easier. Having time alone with Mom and Dad is especially important if a sibling's disability or medical needs take up a great deal of time or energy. A non-disabled or healthy child may resent all the attention his sibling is receiving.

Keep the pride in check. There's nothing wrong with being proud of your gifted child's accomplishments and boasting a bit. But you might want to make sure you're not going overboard, especially in front of another child. Tell your children how proud you are of them but gush in private.

Celebrate everyone's talents and help children support one another. Take time to talk about what makes each family member special. For example, one night at dinner, challenge everyone to name five things they're good at. On a road trip, play "I'm thinking of a person who . . . " and fill in the blanks with an individual's special gifts or skills. Also, if at all possible, bring the whole family to soccer games, band recitals, or school plays so siblings can cheer each other on.

INSIDER TIP

Children who are very close in age often have similar interests. It can be good for siblings to play on the same sports team or participate in the same activity, but if your children are not open to this, don't push the issue. Let children do something they can call their own. Don't put siblings together just because it's easier on you.

Don't allow teasing. Never let a child call his brother or sister "stupid" or say things like, "I'm smarter than you!" For this reason you might want to consider keeping IQ scores to yourself.

Don't compare your children or allow anyone else to do so. Each child is unique and should be treated as such. Saying things like, "When your brother was your age he already knew how to read," only fuels resentful feelings. Be sure teachers are not comparing a younger child to her older sibling, either. A younger child following in an older sibling's bright footsteps may feel as if she can never measure up, so why bother trying.

Finally, don't let giftedness or a disability define your children. Your kids are special for a million reasons. (Ok, maybe two million, but you're prejudiced!) Don't overemphasize grades or let a disability overshadow all the other qualities your child has. This can mean calling your children by name and not referring to them as "the smart one" or "my handful."

Chapter 5

It's a Jungle Gym Out There: Playground Problems

It's a Saturday afternoon and you've taken the kids to the school playground. You're sitting on a bench, off to one side, watching your first grader and an older child by the climber. The older child is scowling at your daughter. Your daughter crosses her arms and says something. The older boy scowls some more. It suddenly becomes clear to you that the older child is preventing your child from going on the slide!

You wait and watch, ready to step in. But a few minutes later, your daughter is happily sliding down the slide after confidently handling the bully on her own.

If the corporate world is a jungle then the school playground is where we learn to deal with all the monkeys.

Bullies

You remember it like it was yesterday—a day at the park, just watching your toddler play. It was a lovely day, when all of a sudden, another toddler wandered over, grabbed the toy from your daughter's hand, and then *WHAM* shoved her down. Your daughter looked over at you with a look that seemed to say, "Help me!" You rushed over to your crying child and whisked her away to safety. Not surprisingly, those protective, don't-mess-with-my-baby feelings don't go away just because your child gets older.

Bullies are a serious issue for kids, parents, and schools. Knowing what a bully is, why they act the way they do, how they pick their victims, and how to respond to them is important information your child can use to protect himself.

What Is a Bully?

Simply put, bullies are people who threaten or hurt others physically, emotionally, or verbally and do so purposefully and repeatedly. In a bully/victim situation there is an imbalance of power or emotion. For example, a bully may be in a higher grade or is calm while his victim is upset.

Why Do Bullies Bully?

Bullies victimize other children for a variety of reasons. Discussing these reasons with your child might help him see bullies in a different light. Looking at a bully as a child with a problem may even help take away some of the bully's power. Reasons children might be bullies include the following: they've been bullied themselves and are modeling behavior they've seen at home or in their neighborhood, they're being pressured by peers to participate in bullying, they've been exposed to excessive violence and are desensitized to it, they're feeling powerless in another setting and are acting out, they lack supervision or have parents who are afraid to discipline, they're jealous of the victim for some reason, they crave attention, or they enjoy having power. Many bullies are good leaders who haven't yet figured out how to get what they want without intimidation.

Do Girls and Boys Bully Differently?

While boys do use verbal threats and put downs to bully another child, they tend to use physical intimidation or abuse as their weapon of choice. For example, boys are more likely to punch, hit, trip, or knock materials out of another child's arms than girl bullies are.

And while girl bullies do, of course, punch, hit, and pull hair, they frequently use psychological warfare to inflict harm. They spread rumors or gossip, stir up problems in relationships, cozy up to a victim and then use information told in confidence to blackmail or humiliate, and socially alienate another child.

Though it's not always the case, bullies tend to victimize those who are the same gender as they are.

How Can I Tell if My Child Is Being Bullied?

Bullies are typically quite skilled at hiding their behavior from adults, choosing to victimize out of the eyesight and earshot of authority or turning on the charm or blaming the victim when caught. And while some kids are open about what's happening, most victims suffer in silence and shame. Chances are, there'll be clues something isn't right. Some signs your child might be a victim of a bully include

- a change in overall mood—a happy, relaxed child is suddenly sad and anxious;
- a loss in appetite;
- physical complaints such as headaches and stomachaches;
- a slip in grades or a new aversion to going to school or riding the bus;

- more requests for lunch money or money for school supplies;
- a new habit of not using the restroom at school;
- coming home hungry—a bully may be taking his lunch money;
- unexplained injuries, torn clothes, or missing property.

What Can I Do to Help My Child?

If your child is being victimized, don't blame him. And DON'T minimize the situation. Take any report of bullying seriously and praise your child for coming to you. Many times, victims wait a long time before finding the courage to step forward. Don't fly off the handle, because your anger may frighten your child or cause him to feel bad about causing upset. Resist the urge to tell your child to fight back. This can be dangerous because the bully may be bigger than your child or there may be a group who is bullying. Telling your child to fight back also says violence is an acceptable way to solve a problem. And resist the urge to tell your child to toughen up. Though it's true bullies tend to target children with low self esteem, a physical difference, or who cry easily, many victims are picked on for no apparent reason. Don't scold your child for tattling. Remember, bullies have the power, and victims often need help to end the abuse.

It is essential you contact your child's teacher and principal about the problem. Because bullies are clever at hiding their behavior, the school needs to be aware of the problem so the situation can be monitored. After you've alerted the school, sit down with your child and together come up with a plan of action. In most cases, the best line of defense for your child to use is to simply ignore the bully or react casually. Tell your child that a good way to appear casual is to put his hands in his pockets and smile. If that doesn't work, your child can try using humor or simply agree with the bully. ("Gee. You're right. My hair does look a little wild today!") Asking a bully why he is bothering you can catch him off guard and defuse the situation. Tell your child he has the right to tell the bully to stop and should do so firmly and clearly. Role-play with your child. Help your child practice saying, "I don't like what you're doing. Stop it now." or "If you do that again, I'm going to go to the teacher." Many times a bully will back down once a victim makes it clear he is not afraid of taking a stand.

If your child is being physically threatened or injured, instruct him to move away immediately, call for help or—if he absolutely has to—defend himself. Explain defending yourself does

WHAT IF MY CHILD IS BEING BULLIED BY A GROUP?

If the abuse is verbal but not physical, tell your child to
- move away if possible.

- stand up to the leader of the group. Suggest to your child that he try humor or logic to diffuse the situation. ("If you keep bullying me, you will get suspended and miss the field trip.") If he can win over the crowd, much of the head bully's power will be taken away.

- look for a friendly face and appeal for help. It often takes only one person or two in the crowd to turn the mood around.

If the abuse is physical, tell your child to
- move away if possible.

- fall to the ground, roll into a ball, and cover her head. One child is no match for a few bullies, let alone a larger group.

- call for help. The crowd may be keeping the teacher or playground supervisor from seeing what's happening. Making noise is the only way to get the attention you need.

If the problem is that the group is ignoring your child, tell your child to
- try to remain or, at least, look calm. Don't give the group what they want by reacting strongly. Read a book, draw, or play with a younger or older student at recess.

- keep talking to those kids with friendly faces. Be patient. One is bound to respond kindly some time.

not mean showering the bully with a flurry of fists. It means momentarily disabling the bully with a shove or stomp on the toes and then moving away to get help.

The old saying about safety in numbers is especially true when it comes to bullies. A child who is being victimized should look

WHAT IF MY CHILD IS A WITNESS TO BULLYING?

Even if your child isn't instigating the abuse or being the victim, she has probably witnessed bullying. Unfortunately, there is often a sort of mob mentality when it comes to bullying. Children panic when someone they know or are friends with begins to bully. They empathize with the victim but don't know how to respond. They become so afraid they'll be next—or get so caught up in the moment—that normally sweet, loving children may stand by while another child is being hurt. What can you do to help your child become a part of the solution instead of the problem?

Encourage your child to stand up. Sometimes all it takes is one, lone voice saying, "Aww, come on. Leave 'em alone," or "Let's do something else," to stop a bully. If your child needs reinforcements, have her recruit another child or two. A few voices are even better than one.

Tell your child to move away. Remind your child that he or she doesn't have to be a part of a bullying crowd. Moving away, and taking a few friends along, can be just as powerful as speaking up.

Suggest to your child that she go get help. Speaking up may be too difficult for some kids. Tell your child that she can help the victim by reporting the bullying. If it's too hard to tell the teacher what's going on, your child can also write a note and pass it along anonymously.

Encourage your child to befriend the victim. Maybe your child couldn't think of anything to do the last time, but there's something he can do about preventing a next time. Encourage your child to ask the bully's victim to join in the game or sit at the lunch table before trouble starts to brew.

for a group to join or one or two friends to hang around with. This advice works well if your daughter is being bullied since girls frequently use group exclusion to inflict harm. Finally, continue to monitor the situation closely, and support your child and the school's efforts. Schools these days have very clear policies about bullying and its consequences, and the majority of the time schools' responses are swift and tough. But it's a good idea to document incidents of bullying in the rare event the school doesn't take the report seriously or isn't successful at stopping the abuse.

What if MY Child Is the Bully?

The teacher calls and says she needs to speak to you about a bullying problem. "I bet it's that shifty, good-for-nothing punk who lives down the street," you think. "What's happened?" you ask and then are shocked to hear your son is not being bullied but doing the bullying!

It's difficult to hear your child is bullying, but it's important you take action.

Try not to get defensive. This is easier said than done, of course, but calmly asking the teacher, principal, or other parent what happened is the best way for you to get all the information you need to see the whole picture. If the other person is using labels or name-calling, say, "Please don't call my child a bully. Talk about what he did."

After you've had a chance to collect your thoughts, talk to your child. Let her know you know what has been going on. Make it clear you love her but that bullying is unacceptable behavior that must stop.

Don't allow your child to blame the victim, saying the other child started it or was asking for it. Encourage your child to start his or her sentences with "I." This will help your child take responsibility for his or her actions and oftentimes provides valuable insight. ("I was mad that Mark always gets to be first in line so I started pushing him down at recess.")

Ask your child if she is being bullied or is having some other trouble that needs to be addressed. Brainstorm together some ways your child could deal with his anger, jealousy, or feelings of powerlessness. If your child is being bullied, as well, contact the school. Your child needs protection, too.

Insist he apologize to his victim. He also needs to pay for any property damage or loss.

SHOULD I CALL THE BULLY'S PARENTS?

Probably not.

As tempting as it is, contacting the parents of your child's bully is typically not a good idea. For one thing, unless you have great restraint, you won't be able to stay calm. For another thing, you're likely to catch the bully's parents off guard, which might cause them to respond defensively or aggressively. Let the school handle the call and resist any suggestion that everyone meet face to face. Having separate conferences means both parties will be able to speak freely. This is true for bully and victim, too. A child who is being bullied shouldn't be forced to sit down with his tormentor to work things out.

If you just can't help yourself or if you know the other parents well enough to confront them or you feel the school hasn't taken your child's complaint seriously, call the other parents only after you're done throwing things and cursing up a storm. Write out or outline what you want to say ahead of time, detailing what has happened to your child. Offer to send photos or other evidence you may have of the abuse or to provide the names of willing witnesses. Avoid accusatory language like "bully" or "thug" or "delinquent." You won't make any allies using these kinds of words! Your goal is to be calm and clear about what you know and what you expect the other parent to do.

Clearly explain what the consequences will be if she is caught bullying again. Possibilities include being grounded or expelled from school. Be prepared to follow through.

Let your child know you will be checking in frequently with his teacher for updates regarding his behavior. Again, follow through.

Be patient. Bullying is a behavior that usually takes some time to change. Consider rewarding your child when she acts appropriately or is making a noticeable effort to improve. Give your child stickers or tokens when he is successful and let him trade them for toys or special outings.

Ask others for help. Unfortunately, many times, teachers, children, and other parents are quick to label a child a "bully" or "troublemaker." Ask those around your child not to use these labels or treat your child as if she will bully. If everyone keeps treating your child as a bully, she will see no point in trying to change.

Sexual Harassment

Sexual harassment is a form of bullying. It is not flirting or the mutual teasing by kids who are figuring out how to respond to the opposite sex, but unwanted and uninvited sexual attention that causes a child's learning or emotional well-being to suffer. While sexual harassment is more prevalent at the junior or high school levels, children in elementary school are at risk as well. At the grade school level, sexual harassment might involve touching, groping, or brushing up against another person; snapping bra straps or pulling down someone's pants or underwear; sharing sexual pictures; using sexual gestures (such as mooning or grabbing your own private areas); calling someone derogatory names (or using "gay" or "lesbian" as an insult); telling dirty jokes; spreading rumors that are sexual in nature; or requesting sexual favors (such as "Show me your breasts!").

As a parent, you can help protect your child from being harassed or harassing another child.

Discus what sexual harassment is with your child. Harassment doesn't have to be physical. And it doesn't have to be a boy/girl situation. Boys can harass other boys (often by name calling) and girls can harass girls (for example, by spreading sexual rumors).

Make sure your child's school has a clear definition and policy regarding sexual harassment. The Department of Education's guidelines regarding sexual harassment allow schools to take into account the age, action, and developmental understanding of children involved when handling a complaint. (A child stealing a kiss from another is one thing in first grade and something quite different in sixth grade.) Still, it's important your child's school has a plan in place. Ask the principal or school counselor to see the policy.

Be a good role model. Don't use sexual slurs or gestures. Respect your children's personal boundaries and teach them to respect each other's privacy. Don't accept unacceptable behavior as a part of growing up or "kids being kids."

Go to the school if you suspect your child is being harassed. As with any form of bullying, try to get as much information as you can about what happened (or is happening). Talk to your child, witnesses, the teacher, the principal. If you decide to file a formal complaint, know that the school must investigate and make temporary arrangements to protect your child. This might include moving your child or the harasser to another classroom or having more adult supervision on the playground.

Cooperate if your child is accused of harassment. Schools must investigate any reports of harassment. Try not to become defensive. If

your child is accused, get his side of the story. Let your child know what action is being questioned and why it's unacceptable. Children in second grade or lower may not be aware they've done anything wrong. Depending on the circumstances, a school may choose to counsel, warn, or suspend a harasser.

When Good Teasing Goes Bad . . .

It's after school and you're waiting for your fifth-grader in the car. You see him off in the distance, waving to another boy. "You blow, Joe!" your normally kind-hearted son calls out.

"And you throw like a girl!" the other boy answers.

Your son piles into the backseat. "What was that?" you ask.

"What? We were just saying good-bye."

Teasing usually gets a bad rap, but it can be a positive thing. Playful and mutual teasing, sometimes called ribbing, is the way children learn to deal with each other, show affection toward one another, and socialize. Boys and girls alike begin to tease early in life. As preschoolers they may begin to use their growing vocabulary to come up with crude or silly insults such as calling someone (occasionally even a parent!) a poop head or goofball. Children in early grades (K–third) often trade similar insults and may begin to play practical jokes on each other. Think about how much delight they take in saying, "There's a monster behind you! Just kidding!" As children grow, their teasing becomes more sophisticated. Children in the older elementary grades love making puns and using word play. For example, adding a twist to someone's name or coming up with "your mama is . . ." or "you're so dumb that . . ." insults. No subject is off limits. Children tease one another about names, physical features, sports abilities, intelligence, and personality traits, among other things.

Of course, when talking about good teasing, playful and mutual are the key words. Unfortunately, it's sometimes difficult for kids to know when teasing crosses the line from fun and harmless to hurtful. You can help keep good teasing from going bad.

Set a good example at home. Don't let teasing get out of hand within your own family. Teach your children teasing stops the moment someone says, "Stop." And don't call your child a pet name or tease them in public.

Help your child read body language. Subtle clues that someone is not enjoying being teased are often lost on kids. This is especially difficult for young children and children with certain special needs such as Asperger's Syndrome. Point out to your child that another child whose mouth is tightly drawn or is standing with his shoulders slumped is probably not having a good time. Reinforce this skill by playing a game where your child tries to guess how you feel by your body language and visa versa.

Encourage your child to speak up. If your child is genuinely hurt by certain taunts, tell him to make his feelings known. Laughing off a hurtful comment will only make things worse.

Never allow your child to tease about physical characteristics. Teasing about a person's physical characteristics or abilities should be off limits. Even if they are made in jest, these remarks can cause self-image problems later on.

Give your child tools for dealing with malicious teasing.
Sometimes children purposefully cross the line and teasing
becomes more of a verbal assault than a playful exchange. If your
child is being bullied, suggest that she first try to act disinter-
ested. Many times, a calm response will take the wind out of a
bully's sails. Kids can also use humor to disarm a bully or have a
quick comeback ready.

Step in if flirting gets out of hand. As children start to go
through puberty, they start to see the opposite sex in a different
light and begin to flirt. Most of the time this flirting is harmless,
entailing things like passing notes, giggling, following each other
around, and calling each other. If attention from the opposite sex
is making your child uncomfortable or interfering with schoolwork, step in. Help your child save face by being the meanie. Tell
your child she can tell friends that you "live in the dark ages" and
won't allow dating until high school. Encourage your child to
throw in some good, old fashioned eye-rolling for added affect.

Friends

You've been anticipating going to an art show
with your eleven-year-old for a month. The
Saturday finally arrives. The two of you are all
set to walk out the door when the phone rings.
It's one of your daughter's friends inviting her
over to play. Your daughter asks if she can blow
off the art show. And that's when it hits you.
You've been replaced.

News flash. You were probably replaced a
while ago and just didn't realize it. Around age
nine or ten, friends seem to replace parents in
children's lives. This is nothing to worry
about; it's natural for pre-adolescent and
adolescent children to pull away. You do want
them to move out on their own someday, don't you?

Like adults, children typically make friends with those who share space with them or who share their interests. Friends are tremendously important. Friends help children figure out their place in the world and how to make their way in it. But things aren't always smooth. Below are some typical troubles relating to friends that may arise in grade school.

Fights

Your child may have so many friends and have so many friendship dramas that you feel as if you're watching a soap opera called "As Emotions Churn." But it doesn't matter if it's the first time or the hundredth time; it's no fun when your child is hurting.

If your child has a falling out with a friend, offer a shoulder to cry on but stay out of it! Listen to your child vent and make general observations, such as "It sounds as if you were having a rough day as friends" or "It can be hard when we fight with friends." If your child is as tight-lipped as Mona Lisa about the fight and making observations isn't getting you anywhere, try making a guess at your child's emotions. "You seem down about the fight," or "I bet you were pretty angry when your friend didn't invite you to the sleepover," might help your child articulate her feelings.

Listen, but whatever you do, don't get caught up in the turmoil or say negative things. You want your child to know you're on her side, but telling her you always thought her best friend was bad news won't help because children's anger is often short-lived. Bite your tongue and consider it preparation for when your teenage daughter dumps her good-for-nothing boyfriend one day and then makes up with him the next day.

Suggest to your child that he and the friend spend a few days apart and take time to calm down. When your child is ready, encourage him to be the first one to pick up the phone or make a peace-offering gesture. (And praise her when she does. It takes a lot of courage to wave the white flag!) Offer to find the art materials needed for your child to make a card or a friendship bracelet to say, "I'm sorry."

If your child and her friend decide to work their differences out in person, resist the urge to play mediator. Create a comfortable space for the children (for example, clear the dining room table so the kids can play a board game and put out

SOME OPEN-ENDED QUESTIONS TO ASK YOUR CHILD WHEN SHE'S HAD A FIGHT WITH A FRIEND

It's best to let children work out their conflicts themselves. Open-ended questions are a good way to get your child thinking about solutions without giving them the answers.

- *Why do you think your friend acted that way?*

- *How did you feel when that happened?*

- *Is there anything you did or said that you wish you hadn't?*

- *Can you think of anything you could do to help your friend feel better?*

- *What would make you feel better?*

- *What would you like to tell your friend if she was here now?*

- *What would you do differently next time?*

snacks) and then make yourself scarce. Leave the room but stay within earshot so you can step in if there are intense (hurt) feelings or things get physical. Leaving the room tells your child and her friend that you're confident they can work things out on their own.

Best Friend Moves Away

Is there anything worse for a kid than seeing a "For Sale" sign in their best friend's yard? Sure there is—a "Sold" sign in their best friend's yard.

In today's highly mobile society, it's quite likely your child will experience this kind of loss at some point. You probably wish you could take away your child's pain altogether, but you can't. There are things you can do, though, to help.

Be a soft place for your child to fall. Losing a friend is a big deal and your child needs your comfort. Don't say things like, "Cheer up. You'll find a new best friend." Your child doesn't care about finding a new best friend; he wants the old one! And don't assume that if your child doesn't mope, cry, or talk about the loss that he is doing fine. Children, especially preadolescents, can have intense but hidden emotions. You can try gentle probing to get your child to open up, saying, for example, "It must have been tough today to watch your best friend load up his things in the moving van." In the days, weeks, and months after the loss, watch your child for signs that he is depressed.

Help your child keep in touch with her friend. You can do this by making arrangements for visits or allowing phone calls. If the best friend has moved out of town, supply your child with stationary and stamps (or give them as a going away present!) An older child might find comfort in an inexpensive calling card so she can call the friend whenever she wants. You can also encourage your child to email her friend as a way to keep in touch.

Encourage your child to cultivate or renew other friendships.
Tell your child that while no one will replace her best friend in
her heart, having a new friend or two to hang around with can
help ease the pain and loneliness. If your child is having a hard
time reaching out, offer to sign her up for a new class or sports
team. Sometimes, classroom cliques are hard to break and a new
setting might help making friends easier.

Three's a Crowd: Friendship Triangles

For some kids, three is definitely a crowd;

"I'm not talking to her anymore! She ditched me even though I
was her friend first."

"I'm her best friend. You're just her second-best friend."

"Choose! It's me or him!"

Relationships change. It can be tough when your child's best
friend since kindergarten suddenly cozies up with someone else
or when a bus buddy starts saving a seat for someone else.
When kids don't have good coping skills, they tend to resort to
the only weapons they can find—withdrawing affection, taunt-
ing, and ultimatums. How can you help if your child is caught in
a friendship triangle?

CHILDHOOD DEPRESSION

*Despite what many people believe, children can and do suffer
from depression. It may not go away on its own. Signs of childhood
depression include, but aren't limited to, persistent sadness (or crying easily or for no apparent reason), withdrawal from family and
friends, talking or drawing about death, a change in eating or
sleeping habits, increased irritability, lack of concentration or a slip
in grades, low energy, and frequent physical complaints such as
stomachaches and headaches. If one or more of these symptoms
have lasted for longer than two weeks and/or are affecting your
child's daily life, contact his or her pediatrician, school counselor, or
another mental health expert right away.*

As with other conflicts with friends, stay out of it. Step in only when your child is being rude or hurtful. For example, if your child has agreed to play with one friend, don't let him change his mind to appease another friend.

Model good friendships. If your friend can't go out to lunch with you, don't complain. And when the opportunity presents itself, point out to your child that each of your friends is special and brings something to your life. Perhaps one friend is a "movie buddy," or another goes to the gym with you or is the one you call when you want to talk politics.

Support your child by helping her articulate her feelings. Comments such as "It sounds as if you really miss your friend today," or "So you're feeling left out? A little jealous?" can be just the thing a wounded heart needs.

Help your child improve his coping skills. Dealing with someone who is "intruding" on a friendship with another person is tough for kids. There are many things you can suggest to your child to help ease the hurt feelings or improve the situation. For example, your child could write in a journal, count to ten when the other child interrupts a game or conversation, invite the new friend over to get to know him better, or invite the old friend over for some special one-on-one time.

Shyness

For some children, having one or two special playmates is plenty. There's nothing wrong with this. Just because you may be a social butterfly doesn't mean your child can't be a caterpillar. It's when your child doesn't have any friends or wants more friends and doesn't know what to do, that it's time to step in.

Children who have trouble making friends are often shy. How can parents help? First, don't label your child. If you continually refer to your child as the "shy one" or make excuses for her, such as "Don't mind her, she's shy" when she won't say hello, your child will believe those labels and act accordingly. Second, let your child know there's nothing wrong with her being scared; it's how we respond to our fears that matter. Let her know you believe in her ability to face and overcome her shyness. And third, help your child practice forging friendships with role-play. Encourage her to start small. The easiest way to make a friend is to smile and ask questions. Help your child prepare some answers, too. Nothing kills a conversation quicker than saying, "Uh, I don't know," when someone asks you what subject you like best or what your favorite music group is. If things go well, suggest to your child he or she invite a new friend to do something they both enjoy. Whatever you do, don't push your child. Let her work at her own pace and at her own comfort level. Inviting over all the girls in her class for a surprise tea party the first week of school? Not a good plan.

Though many kids who struggle to make friends are shy, kids may have trouble making friends for other reasons. Maybe they have undiagnosed hearing or language problems, making communication with other children difficult. Maybe they are gifted and don't relate to children their own age or are afraid of classmates' reactions to their abilities. Or perhaps they behave in a way or have nasty habits that turn off other kids. For example, they're bossy, smelly, pick their nose with abandon, or are overly sensitive. In these situations, parents need to gently pinpoint the problem and address the issues. If your child is bossy, you could say something like, "I've noticed you're having trouble making as many friends as you want. I was wondering if that's because you like to be in charge all the time" (or can't hear, understand other kids, cry easily, etc.). If the direct method gets you nowhere, you might have to go stealth. For example, buy your child her own deodorant and leave it on the bathroom sink with a note that says, "Use me!" or pack some tissues in your child's backpack.

Running with the Wrong Crowd

In a perfect world, your child would have perfect friends, the kind who say "please" and "thank you," get top marks in school, remember to wipe their feet at the door, and, every once in awhile,

---

THE OUTSIDER

It's morning and your daughter slides into the kitchen wearing mismatched clothes, a tiara, and purple snow boots. (It's spring.) There's no point in asking her if that's what she intends to wear to school—you already know it is.

There always seems to be one in every class—one child who is different than the other children. One who stands off or out because of the way he dresses, thinks, or spends time. A child considered an outsider. There's nothing wrong, of course, with being different. And some children are quite comfortable marching to their own beat. But if your child is hurting because his unique personality is keeping classmates away, it can break your heart to watch. How can you help?

Accept and love your child unconditionally. Don't try to squash your square peg into a round hole. Celebrate your child's differences— even if they embarrass you or make you uncomfortable. Your "outsider" needs to know he is a loveable and worthwhile human being. The more self confidence and self esteem your child has, the easier it will be for her to withstand the hard knocks being unconventional can bring.

Help your child find her niche. School may not be the place your child fits in, so find out where she does fit in. Is your child into theater? Enroll her in acting classes. Is she into writing? Find a writing group or help her start her own. The important thing is your child has someplace or a group of friends where she feels accepted.

compliment you on your good housekeeping. Unfortunately, perfect friends don't exist. From the beginning of time, parents have been trying to pick who their children are friends with and children have been bringing home playmates their parents can't stand.

So how should you respond if your child is friends with someone you're not crazy about? First, ask yourself, "Is this relationship dangerous? Or do I just find this other kid annoying?"

If the other child is encouraging yours to do things that jeopardize his safety or well-being, don't tolerate the friendship! Such things might include verbal or physical abuse, shoplifting or vandalizing, playing with weapons or fire, exploring abandoned houses or train tracks, or trying drugs. There is nothing more important than your child's safety. Though it may be tempting to forbid your child from ever seeing the other child, resist the urge. Forbidding will only make the friendship more appealing. Instead, sit down with your child and make it clear why you object to his friendship with the other child. Tell him a real friend would never endanger him or ask him to do things that would get him in trouble. Keep your child and the other child close to home, where you can keep an eye on their activities. If you can, provide your child (of any age!)

INSIDER TIP

Age and gender play a role in friendships. For example, while younger children (those eight and under) can certainly have strong attachments, their friendships seem to be shorter-lived and less emotionally intense than the friendships of older children. And while girls express their affection in intimate ways, such as conversation and sharing secrets, boys tend to express their feelings physically, through rough play or joking around with one another. Another noticeable difference between boys and girls is that girls tend to interact with a small circle of friends while boys hang out in crowds.

with a two-way radio or cell phone he can use to call you if he gets into a situation he doesn't know how to deal with and needs to be picked up.

If the other child is not a troublemaker but just rubs you the wrong way, there's not much you can do. Respect your child's choice; you may not see any redeeming qualities in the other child but your child does. You never know when little ears are listening, so never badmouth the friend. (And save the eye rolls for when you're alone.) Be pleasant and patient. One of two things will happen. Either the kid will grow on you or the friendship will eventually end. No. Wait. There's another possible scenario. Your son and his buddy could end up being close for the rest of their lives. Just in case, start practicing how to smile through gritted teeth so you'll be ready when the young man gives an obnoxious toast at your son's wedding!

Do Crushes Hurt? Check One: Yes __ No __

It's a strange phenomenon. One day your son is talking about cooties and the next, he's talking about his girlfriend! The 180-degree shift can make your head spin.

Boyfriend-girlfriend stuff always seems to start sooner than parents want or expect, so be prepared. Starting around age eleven or twelve (right around the time those darn hormones kick in!) your child may experience her first crush and, consequently, her first broken heart.

At this age, children are just beginning to dip their feet into the water of Lake Opposite Sex. They "go out" but rarely does this mean they actually spend time together. In fact, both sides are usually so nervous they don't even talk to one another! Instead, communications are handled through friends. "Agents" even do the breaking up when the time comes. Boys and girls like to pass a lot of notes with boxes that say things like, "Do you think this will work out between us? Check Yes or No." (This is hard to decide when notes are signed Anonymous!) But just because these relationships are awkward and brief doesn't mean your child isn't heartbroken when they end.

"I'M GOING TO MARRY MISS KELLY!"

For two weeks all you've heard is Miss Kelly said this, Miss Kelly did that. It's bad enough you're feeling your spotlight is fading a bit, but then your son comes home and announces that when he's grown up, he's going to marry his teacher. You remember when your son was five and wanted to marry you!

All children are prone to "falling in love" with their teachers. Like crushes on peers, crushes on teachers are generally short lived, ending quickly once the teacher does something offending, like mentioning her significant other or giving two pages of extra homework. Most times these endings are relatively painless, but they can hurt, too. If your child's heart was broken by Teacher, offer a shoulder to cry on or try a little humor. Ask him if he'd really want to marry someone who'd make him practice multiplication tables every night.

FRIENDSHIPS BETWEEN BOYS AND GIRLS

"There's no one to hang out with!" your fifth-grader complains one Saturday.

"Why don't you call up your friend Shannon?" you suggest, remembering how much fun your son and neighbor had playing countless games of Monopoly.

"Are you serious?!" your son replies. *"She's a girl now!"*

Hasn't she always been a girl? you wonder.

When children are babies and preschoolers, they couldn't care less what gender their friends are. Somewhere around kindergarten or first grade, children begin to notice differences and segregate themselves as they learn to identify with being a boy or a girl. Despite this natural division, most children continue to be friends. In other words, gender isn't a deal breaker when it comes to relationships! Things change, though, when children become preadolescents (nine to twelve years old) and hormones start to churn. Kids who were once inseparable friends find themselves on opposite sides of the room. Sometimes it's the general awkwardness of puberty getting in the way of boys and girls continuing their friendships. More often than not, though, boy-girl friendships are nixed because of social pressure. This is too bad because boys and girls can benefit greatly from having friends of the opposite sex. For example, these friendships help children see the world from a different perspective and practice adult interactions in a non-sexual way.

How can you help your child deal with the loss of a friend or nurture friendships with members of the opposite sex?

Ask, listen, and validate. Your child may be anxious to talk about the loss of a boy or girl friend. Or your child may want to vent about how unfair it is that he can't even talk with a girl without everyone singing about him and the girl "sitting in a tree, k.i.s.s.i.n.g." Acknowledge any hurt and disappointed feelings and let your child know you understand.

Don't tease or sing the "sitting in the tree" song yourself. *If a girl calls your son, don't get silly, wink, or otherwise make an issue of it. And don't allow siblings to tease either. This kind of behavior only fuels the myth that boys and girls can't be friends.*

Be the fun mom or dad. *Do your child and his classmates a favor by giving them a good excuse to hang out together. Offer to host a game or video night at your home or an outing to an arcade, movie, or skating rink. This way, kids can enjoy each other's company in a casual setting. But don't forget—these are preadolescents and prone to stupid behavior. Lay down the ground rules, set limits, and supervise!*

Reassure your child. *If nothing else, reassure your child that someday it will be no big deal to have friends of the opposite sex. By the time they're in high school, most children are comfortable once again with the idea of having friends who are the opposite sex and understand platonic relationships are possible.*

How can parents take the sting out of Cupid's arrow? The best thing you can do is listen with a sympathetic ear. It may be "just a crush" or puppy love to grownups but it's a big deal to your child. It hurts and your child needs a soft place to fall. Let her cry her eyes out if she needs to and then assure her she will feel a little better each day. Tell her about one or two broken hearts you've survived; it might help her feel as if someone understands what she's going through and that there is light at the end of the tunnel. If your child is responding with anger instead of tears, let him know you will help him find a safe way to vent those painful feelings.

Peer Pressure

You've had the same conversation a half-dozen times already this week.

"But whyyyy can't I go to the movie?" your son asks. "All my friends watch PG–13 shows."

"And if all your friends jumped off a cliff, would you do it too?" you say.

Without missing a beat your son answers. "Yes!"

Peer pressure is a powerful thing. Though it intensifies in the teenage years, children in elementary school struggle, too. Not all peer pressure is bad. For instance, children may feel challenged to study if their friends are doing well in school or be more willing to participate in a recess game if everyone else is playing. But when children are pressured into doing something they are uncomfortable with, that goes against their values, or that they know is wrong—that's when parents should worry.

Children give into peer pressure for a variety of reasons: they want to be liked, they want to fit in, they're afraid of ridicule, they're curious. As a parent, you can help children stand up to the challenge of negative peer pressure:

Be a good role model. Children take their cue from watching Mom and Dad, so don't give in to peer pressure yourself. Don't buy the latest car or gadget to "Keep up with the Jones." And don't allow your child to do something or buy something only because his or her peers are or because your child is pestering you. (Occasionally giving in and buying the latest fashion or CD everyone has respects your child's need for a sense of belonging. As long as you're not compromising your own family values, a rare, little indulgence won't harm your child.)

Warn your child about peer pressure. Talk with your child about some of the situations they are likely to encounter so they can be ready to deal with them.

Role play. Ask your child "What if . . . " and let him practice his response. Brainstorm possible replies or actions your child could take if they were feeling pressured. Don't just role play once. Review and practice every few months.

Know your child's friends. This will make it easier for you to help your child avoid situations where negative peer pressure would be a problem.

Remind your child of your family's values and stand up for your own beliefs. Your child may not always follow your family values, but at least he will know where you stand. Be clear and consistent in your expectations.

SOME "WHAT IFS?" TO ASK YOUR CHILD

- What if some of your friends were talking about skipping school?

- What if a bunch of kids were picking on another student?

- What if your friend wanted to cheat off your homework paper?

- What if you went to a sleepover and everyone wanted to watch a movie you knew you weren't allowed to see?

- What if someone was trying to get you to try a cigarette? Take a sip of beer? Take a pill?

- What if a group of friends called you a sissy for wearing a bike helmet?

- What if none of your friends wanted to go Trick-or-Treating but you still did?

- What if some boys in your class were pulling out paper towels, running the water, and making a mess in the school bathroom?

- What if some friends wanted to talk to you but it was time to listen to the teacher?

Listen but don't judge. Don't freak out if your son comes home telling you about a friend who got his ear pierced over the weekend. Maybe your son wants to see how you'd respond if he asked you to take him to get his ear pierced. Listening without judgment will keep communication lines open.

Praise your child. Children with good self esteem are less likely to fall prey to negative peer pressure. Look for opportunities to build your child's self esteem, encourage him to be a good leader, and praise him when he makes a good choice. For example, "I noticed that even though your teammates were being bad sports, you shook hands with the player on the opposing team who scored the winning goal. You should be proud of yourself. I'm proud of you."

When Kids Don't Click

Your fourth grader climbs into the car after school huffing and puffing. "What's wrong?" you ask.

"We have to do a science project!"

"Oh, my goodness," you say. "The teacher is making you work? How terrible."

"And that's not all," your daughter says, ignoring your sarcasm. "We have to have partners and I got stuck with Alison!"

Having to work with people you don't like is a part of life. But just because your child has to work with someone she would never choose as a friend, doesn't mean her life—or the other child's—has to be miserable. If your child comes home complaining about a classmate, look at it as a great opportunity to teach tolerance.

First of all, let your child know it's okay not to like everyone. It simply isn't realistic to think you'll get along with everybody, all the time. Without naming names, share your experiences with your child. Is there someone at work you can't stand? How do

---

IF IT'S PREJUDICE . . .

Not wanting to work with someone because you don't like her personality is one thing. Not wanting to work with someone because they are a different color, religion, ethnicity, or have a physical or developmental difference is something else altogether—prejudice.

Children learn prejudice by watching. If you want to raise a child who doesn't discriminate, be a good role model:

- *Discuss prejudice at an early age, which is when children notice differences in people. There is nothing wrong with noticing differences (though you wish they'd notice a little quieter at times!) but making judgments about a person based on their color, nationality, physical appearance, sex, or religion is not okay.*

- *Watch your language. Don't make racial, cultural, or other kinds of slurs—even in jest. And if your child sees any on television or in other media, use it as an opportunity to discuss why these labels are hurtful.*

- *Value and celebrate uniqueness within your family and in your neighborhood. Go to your Vietnamese neighbor's house for dinner. Buy your niece a Chanukah gift though your family celebrates Christmas.*

- *Learn about other groups and their traditions. Take advantage of cultural events in your community.*

you handle it? Maybe you deal with the person you don't like first thing in the morning so you get it out of the way. Brainstorm some ideas your child could use. (For example, smiling to change your mood, making sure you work with the person when you're not cranky, asking a friend to keep you company when you have to work with the person.)

Second, let your child know that while it's okay to dislike a person, everyone deserves kindness and respect. Tell your daughter you will not tolerate her mistreating or badmouthing a classmate.

Third, help your child see the big picture. Every person, every interaction can be an opportunity to learn and grow. Your child may dislike a classmate, but that classmate has something worthwhile to contribute or share. Encourage your child to look for something she learned from the other person or for something she can appreciate. Alison isn't the person your daughter would like to invite to come spend the night, but maybe she's a hard worker or knows a lot about the science topic. Along the same lines, encourage your child to find one thing she and her classmate have in common, even if it's as simple as hating science homework. Having at least one safe conversation topic can help when you're stuck with someone you don't like.

And finally, don't let your child talk you into insisting the teacher allow her to change partners. Remind your child she'll have to deal with this other person for a relatively short time. The science project will be over in two weeks. The teacher will assign new seats next quarter. The school year will be over in nine months.

Chapter 6

"Mom, My Project's Due Tomorrow!": Handling Homework

You're in the living room, sitting in your favorite easy chair when your son waltzes in. "Mom, how much do you weigh?"

"Excuse me?" you say and put down the brownie you're eating. You decide to change the subject. "Why aren't you doing your homework?"

"This is my homework!" your daughter explains. "I'm supposed to ask everyone in my family how much they weigh and convert the pounds to kilograms." Mama Mia, you think. What ever happened to good, old-fashioned worksheets?

While the types of homework may have changed over the years, homework itself has always been an issue in many households. Whether your child's school believes in loading kids down with work, has a "no homework" policy, or falls somewhere in between, homework headaches require more than a couple of aspirin.

How Much Homework?

Too Much Homework

There's no such thing as too much of a good thing—unless it's homework and your child is up to her ear lobes in it every night.

Too much homework can cause stress. Lots of it. A child who routinely has too much homework can become overwhelmed, frustrated, and driven to tears or other emotional outbursts. She may become resentful toward school if too much homework is keeping her from the things she loves, like playing sports. She may even be tempted to cheat to get all her homework done. Too much homework can stress parents, too. According to the National Parent-Teacher Organization, a good rule of thumb is ten minutes of homework per grade. For example, if your child is in the second grade, she should be doing no more than 20 minutes of work each night. A fifth grader should expect no more than 50 to 60 minutes a night. Anything more and homework assignments are a burden and counterproductive to learning.

If your child has to ice down her writing hand each night, the first thing to do is make sure your daughter isn't struggling in a particular subject. Sometimes, kids who are feeling lost will procrastinate, allowing assignments to pile up, or spend so much time on one subject that they fall behind in others. To determine what's going on, ask your child flat out if she's having a difficult time or sit down with her and watch her work. Is she frustrated, unusually irritable, or easily distracted? These may be signs she's struggling.

Next, find out if it's an organizational problem. Ask your daughter how much time she had to complete the assignments at school: you may find out your daughter is spending her time daydreaming instead of working. You might want to talk to parents of other children in your daughter's class, too. See if their kids are bringing home a ton of work each night.

Once you've determined whether your child is having trouble or is simply one of many feeling overloaded, talk to the teacher. Teachers can do a lot of things but they can't read minds. They want to know if a student is having trouble and most will step

S.O.S. STUDENT OVERLOADED AND OVERWHELMED!

A child who is so overwhelmed by homework that he is tearful, throwing books, or crumpling papers is not learning. Vowing to talk to the teacher the next day is a good idea but what can you do to help your child now, in the middle of homework overload meltdown?

First, insist your child take a break. When emotions run high, it's difficult to think straight or be reasonable. Tell your child she needs to stop, put the homework aside, and do something else—anything else!—for at least ten to fifteen minutes or until she is feeling calm again. Doing something physical, such as going for a bike ride or dancing to music, is a good way to relieve pent-up stress.

Second, offer emotional support. When your child is ready to sit down and try again, join him or her at the desk or table. You don't have to be actively involved in helping with the work; your child may draw strength just from having you nearby. If your child requests help, calmly review what the homework assignment is and ask things like, "What have you done so far? What part is giving you the most trouble?" Your goal is to get your child focused once again on the assignment without taking over and bailing him out.

And finally, give your child permission to stop. If, after a certain amount of time, your child is still frustrated and overwhelmed by the amount of work or the assignment, give her permission to call it a day (or night). Thirty minutes is a fair amount of time for most elementary students. If your child is worried about the incomplete assignment, reassure her you are going to write a note to the teacher. And then do it. In the note, explain what happened, how you and your child tried to remedy the situation, and ask if your child may have more time to complete the assignment. If not, explain you and your child are prepared to accept the consequences.

INSIDER TIP

Some teachers already have a "thirty-minute" homework rule. In other words, they allow students—who have given a genuine effort—to stop working on homework after thirty minutes (or after another predetermined, appropriate amount of time), regardless if the assignment is finished. If your child is routinely overwhelmed by homework, consider approaching his teacher with this idea. It can be a great compromise for teachers and students.

back and reevaluate their homework policy or expectations if enough parents complain about the workload being consistently too heavy. If, however, you've approached your child's teacher about the amount of homework she requires and nothing is done, it's time to take your concerns to the principal. If your child is under a great deal of stress because of an overload of homework, you might also enlist the support of the school counselor when you talk to the teacher and principal.

Too Little Homework

At first glance, a no homework policy may appear to be a busy family's dream come true. It's definitely a kid's dream come true! And while dividing your day into school and home and rarely mixing the two can be a positive experience, this increasingly popular approach also has a couple of downsides.

One of these downsides is that children who are struggling do not have enough time to practice and improve their skills. Without an occasional outside assignment, teachers and parents may miss that a child didn't understand fractions the first time around or never learned to read a graph. For some children, working on assignments at home—where a parent can give his or her full attention to helping—may be what a struggling student needs.

Another downside to a schoolwide no homework policy is that children don't learn how to organize their time or study outside of school. What happens when a child who's never had much homework moves to a new school and suddenly has a teacher who piles it on? Or what happens when a fifth grader goes to middle school and is expected to do homework for several subjects every night? A happy balance is essential.

If you feel your child would benefit from more homework, speak with the teacher and ask her to send work home. (Just don't let your child hear you; she's not likely to appreciate it!) Explain you're not looking for busy work but meaningful practice or ways to expand what's been taught during the school day. Of course, you can always supplement classroom work with projects you and your child come up with on your own. Was your son's curiosity peaked during a class lesson on biodegradable materials? Encourage your child to write a brochure for neighbors on the importance of recycling. Did your daughter enjoy the chapter book read in class? Help her locate the sequel at the library.

Meaningless Homework

Sometimes the problem isn't that there's too much or too little homework; it's that the homework doesn't seem to have a meaningful purpose. If your child is bringing home what you consider "busy work," speak up! Ask your child's teacher what purpose the

INSIDER TIP

Parents can go a long way in heading off problems by talking to teachers at the beginning of the year. Ask, How much homework can my child expect each night? Do you want parents to help? What types of homework do you assign? Will my child have any long-term projects? What are the consequences if my child doesn't complete her homework on time? What happens if my child can't complete her homework because of family commitments that are beyond her control? Can this work be made up? What's the best way to contact you if my child is having trouble with the work?

work is serving. Her answer should be something along the lines of to help students review or practice skills learned in the classroom, to help children get ready for the next day's lesson, to teach them to use a new resource such as a dictionary or the Internet, or to expand on a subject. Homework should never be used to punish kids. If you don't get a satisfactory answer, talk to the principal.

Getting It Done

Healthy Homework Habits

Healthy homework habits don't just happen. They need a helping hand:

Provide a quiet, well-lit space with few distractions. You don't need a desk; the kitchen table will do if it's away from the TV and radio.

Make sure all necessary materials are handy. A child who has to track down a sharpened pencil, paper, or a dictionary is easily distracted.

Make homework time part of your routine. Some families have a rule that homework is to be done right after school or right after dinner. (Too close to bedtime may not be a good idea, though first thing in the morning may work for some kids who are early risers.) Other families have a "work first, play later" rule. Find a system that works for your family and stick to it.

Be available. You don't need to hover over your child, but be around if she needs help.

Look over your child's assignments when she's finished. Check answers but don't fix errors—unless the teacher wants parents to go over mistakes and rework problems together, which, often, they do. Remember, this is your child's homework, not yours.

SOME SIGNS YOU'RE OVERINVOLVED WITH YOUR CHILD'S HOMEWORK

You want to help your child, but knowing how much help is too much can be tricky at times. Here are some red flags that it's time to put the pencil down and step away from the homework area:

- *You sit down to help your child every night or sit down without being asked.*

- *You constantly nag your child to do his homework. Homework is your child's responsibility. If you've given him two warnings and he doesn't sit down and do it, let the chips fall where they may.*

- *You feel yourself getting frustrated while helping. If you raise your voice or roll your eyes or pound the table more than three times consider that your cue to take a hike.*

- *You are still working on the homework assignments long after your child has lost interest or gone to bed.*

- *You are doing more work (gathering materials, doing research, etc.) than your child is.*

- *Your child is telling you to "Go away! Leave me alone."*

- *You say, "What did we get?" when your child brings home graded work!*

Perfectionism

Your daughter's homework is to rewrite a fairy tale. She's been working on it for over an hour. Every few minutes she writes something down, reads it, and then promptly erases her work. She's in tears, her eraser is in shreds, and you're ready to scream, "For the love of Pete! Just write something! Anything!"

Watching your child battle perfectionism can cause you to feel, well, like being a less-

WHAT IF I DON'T UNDERSTAND THE HOMEWORK?

Your six-year-old gets all excited because she's made a text-to-text connection. Your nine-year-old is frustrated because he's having trouble with regrouping. You're just wondering what the heck is going on!

Don't worry. You haven't suddenly lost brain cells. Plenty of smart parents get confused when it comes to helping their child with homework. Sometimes it's a matter of forgetting how to do something. (You never could remember the mathematical order of operations, could you?) Other times, it's a matter of not being up on current, educational buzz words. For example, a text-to-text connection means reading one book makes you think of another; regrouping is what once was known as carrying over or borrowing.

If you are having trouble understanding your child's homework, you have several options: ask other parents, consult a homework help line, ask the teacher to explain the work or to offer a parent workshop so everyone can learn the classroom approaches, or sneak a peek at your child's textbook when he's asleep and brush up. Of course, you could use the old standby—pretend you already know the subject and tell your child you just want to make sure he knows it so please explain it to you. Hey, you never know. It might work.

than-perfect parent. But as frustrating as it is for parents, perfectionism is worse on kids. Perfectionists impose rigid and unrealistic goals for themselves. They are highly critical of themselves and, frequently, of others. For whatever reason, they base their self-worth on achievement and are so afraid of failing or disappointing others that they are sometimes paralyzed, unable to complete or even begin a project. Being a perfectionist is different than being ambitious. Ambitious people are highly driven but receive genuine satisfaction from hard work and success. Perfectionists are never happy, never satisfied with their work. Left unchecked, perfectionism can lead children to poor self esteem, depression, pessimism, obsessive behavior, and failing school.

If your child is a perfectionist or heading down that road, here are some ways you can help:

Be a good role model. Perfectionism is frequently a learned trait. If you're a perfectionist, lighten up on yourself. Telling your child her homework doesn't have to be perfect when you're killing yourself, working late into the night putting together the "perfect report" for work, is pointless. Children are much better observers than listeners.

Be mindful of the way you respond to your child's success. If, for example, your child comes home with a B don't let the first thing you ask her be "Why didn't you get an A?" If you're never satisfied with your child's performance, how can you ever expect her to be?

Help your child set attainable goals and encourage her to change her idea of success. If your child is stressing about acing a test, encourage her to be happy with a 90 percent. Maybe winning the state spelling bee is not likely, but qualifying to go in the first place is a worthy goal. Be prepared for some resistance. Setting reasonable standards is a tough thing for perfectionists to do. They want to be the best, not just do their best.

Encourage her to focus on the process and not the end product. Having the best fairy-tale story in the class doesn't matter. Enjoying the writing process is more important. Tell your child she can quiet her inner critic by working without stopping to revise or saying out loud, "I'm having fun!"

Set time limits. When your perfectionist sits down to work, set a timer with a reasonable amount of time to complete the job. This can help kids who complete work, but then spend hours revising, redoing or rechecking an assignment. You might even try taking the work away once it's complete.

Celebrate mistakes. Mistakes are great opportunities to learn. They are also a great opportunity to laugh. Instead of berating herself for not seeing the extra credit question, encourage your child to say, "Whoops! Who knew questions like to hide on the back of tests?"

Encourage her to take risks. One of the best ways to learn to deal with mistakes is to make them! Encourage your child to try something new, something you know will challenge her, and then reward her effort. Get into the act yourself by taking those piano lessons you always wanted or trying a new, complicated recipe.

Procrastination

One night, around 9:00 your son tells you he can't go to sleep yet. "Sure you can," you say. "You just crawl in bed and close your eyes . . ."

"But Moooom!" your son says. "My project is due tomorrow!"

Yikes! Now what? Whether you allow your child to stay up late to work on the project, send him to school without the work and let him suffer the consequences, do the project for him, or call him in sick the next day is up to you as a parent. There are no good solutions. (Though sending your child to school without the work to suffer the consequences is probably the best way to prevent future last-minute project disasters.) Chalk it up as yet one more adventure in parenting and then aim your sights on preventing procrastination the next time. If your child is famous for putting off today what he has to turn in tomorrow, here's a step-by-step plan.

Step one. As soon as an assignment is made, have your child sit down and come up with a doable work schedule. You may have to walk your older child through this step the first couple of times. After that, tell him scheduling/planning is strictly his job. Younger students will probably need more guidance when it comes to setting up a work schedule. Developmentally, children in grades two and below have difficulty estimating time. Have your child list all his commitments such as piano lessons and soccer practice and holidays. (Have your child include time to play and relax, too!) Ask your child how long he thinks it will take to do each task and have him record the amount of time beside the tasks. For example, Go to library and check out books: One afternoon. Write the opening paragraph: thirty minutes. Next, suggest to your child he write the schedule out on a chart to keep in a highly visible place.

Step two. Sometimes the biggest problem is just getting started, so have your child pick a date to begin. By choosing a no-excuses-this-is-when-I'm-starting date, the pressure to begin is off and there's less time for a procrastinator to get sidetracked. Letting your child choose the date is important; it helps him take responsibility for doing the work and meeting his own deadlines. If your child picks a wildly late date, sit down and go over his work schedule with him. Point out any unrealistic task or time goals without making obvious judgments. For example, you might say, "Do you think it will be possible to make it to the library that day? What about your early soccer practice?" or "Two days to do the whole project? Hmmm. That's a lot of work to do in a short time." Resist the urge to do the scheduling yourself. Your goal should be to get your child to practice good time-management skills.

Step three. Once the project is started, encourage your child to work only on what's on the schedule. Sticking to the task at hand will help keep your child from becoming overwhelmed or burning

INSIDER TIP

If your child feels success right at the beginning, he'll be more motivated to keep working. Encourage your child to keep the first day of working on a project simple. Make the goal to gather all the materials or pick a title and write an opening paragraph or some other fairly easy task.

out—both of which might cause him to lose momentum. This is especially true for younger children who tire more quickly and often are more easily frustrated than older students. Of course, if your child finishes the work for the night and wants to keep working . . . well, don't throw water on the fire! How long he works should be his decision.

Step four. Suggest your child give himself some "worry time." Most procrastinators are perfectionists and so afraid of failing they simply can't bring themselves to work at a reasonable pace. In order to counterbalance this, tell your child he has exactly ten minutes (or whatever amount of time your child feels he needs) to revise, plan, or fret about how the project is going to turn out and then that's it. Let your child set a timer if you need to. More often than not, getting the worrying out of the way will help a procrastinator concentrate when it's time to work.

Disorganization

You have to pick up your daughter early so you write a note to school. The only thing is, when you go to put it in her backpack you can't find her folder. You find a lot of other interesting things, though. Crumpled notes, stray worksheets, and a half-eaten peanut butter sandwich. (Thankfully it's still in its baggie!) "How can you find anything in this mess?!" you ask your daughter as you dump out

the contents of the backpack on the
kitchen table.

"Moooom! Now you've messed it
all up!"

Sound familiar?

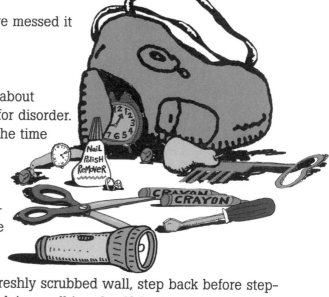

Many parents worry about
their children's love for disorder.
Fortunately, most of the time
there's no cause for
alarm. After all, one
person's mess is
another person's sys-
tem. If your son is the
poster child for stu-
dent slobs and it's
driving you up your freshly scrubbed wall, step back before step-
ping in. Is your child doing well in school? Is she able to find
what she needs, when she needs it? Are her things in fairly good
condition? If so, don't worry. Obviously, your child is comfortable
and functioning well in her mess. If the disarray is making you
dizzy with stress, insist your child at least keep her things in a
confined area, preferably some place with a door you can close!
If, however, your child's lack of organizational skills is interfering
with her schoolwork, it's time to offer a little guidance.

First, provide organizational materials or tools. Offer to buy your
child color-coded pocket folders or a wire basket where she can
put her assignments. A desk or a drawer just for her might inspire
her to put away work. Some children find a weekly calendar or a
spiral notebook helpful in keeping track of homework or long-
term projects.

If your child is a younger student or a non-reader, use containers
with picture labels. (Print the label below the picture to help
improve reading skills.) You can also use picture labels on a large
calendar to help children keep track of what classes they have

each day or assignments that are due. If you're going to provide your young student with a notebook to keep track of assignments, get one that's on the small side. Small notebooks are more manageable for small hands.

Next, get your child into the habit of going through her notebook and/or backpack every afternoon and tossing anything she doesn't need. Have a special place to put papers that are a priority. If it's too hard for your child to prioritize, set aside what you know is important and challenge your child to get rid of at least half of what's left. (Younger kids often have a harder time than older ones deciding what's worth keeping.) Keep the papers for several weeks, and then bring them out and try again. Ask your child, "Did you need this after all? Is this still important?" After a few times, your child will hopefully begin to make better choices.

Establish a "once a week" rule when it comes to your child cleaning out her desk or workspace. This will help your child to stay on top of the mess and make it easier to organize materials.

And finally—and most importantly—make organization your child's responsibility. Remember, you can lead a child to the new containers and notebook you bought her but you can't make her use them. If you want your child to see the value of good organization, let her suffer the consequences or enjoy the rewards of her actions.

Chapter 7

Extra Credit:
A Few More Snafus

So, you've passed the tests. You breezed through most of the questions, stumbled on a few others and had to go back over your notes. On one or two of the problems you just guessed and hoped for the best. Now, it's time for a little extra credit.

Did you miss Spring Fever in your School Handbook? How about Art Avalanches or Teacher Gifts? Don't be surprised. They weren't there; they are the kinds of trials that pop up now and then when you least suspect it (and usually when you can least spare the time). Don't panic; your kids are just trying to make sure you're paying attention. If you don't let them see you sweat, you're home free.

"We Want You!"

Volunteering at School

It's open house night at your children's school and everywhere you look there are sign-up sheets. Sign up to be our class parent! Sign up to help with our field trip! Sign up to bring snacks next week! Sign up to be on the yearbook committee! You'd like to help, but you're not sure where to start.

Parent volunteers are a vital part of any school community. They bring valuable skills, excitement, and a fresh perspective to classrooms and improve the education of all students. Parent volunteers also bring a tremendous sense of community to schools, demonstrating to children that they and their education are important. Being a volunteer can mean you are more aware of the goings-on at your child's school (or in her classroom), which can make dealing with any problems or concerns easier. So if volunteering is so rewarding and important, what keeps parents from doing it?

I Don't Have Anything to Offer

Many parents believe they have no skills or talents to offer or that the amount of time they can volunteer is too small to be helpful. Nothing could be further from the truth. There are hundreds of ways parents can help in their child's school. And while some require a bigger time commitment than others, ALL are greatly appreciated by teachers and school staff.

I Want to Volunteer But Can't

Work schedules as well as having a baby or other commitments at home can make volunteering during the school day impossible. If you're in this position, take heart. There are still plenty of ways you can support your child's school or the staff. For example, there are many volunteer opportunities that can be carried out at home or after kids are in bed: making phone calls, cutting construction paper for art projects, typing up the class newsletter, baking, or collecting

PARENT VOLUNTEER JOBS

• Listen to kindergartners or first graders read out loud.

• Help students find their way to their classrooms on the first day.

• Monitor bus drop off, the playground, or the lunchroom.

• Sell snacks in the lunchroom.

• Staple, copy, collate, or laminate papers for teachers.

• Chaperone field trips.

• Call local businesses for donations for a fundraiser.

• Host a teacher appreciation lunch or cook for such a luncheon.

• Shelve library books.

• Hang student work around the school for the art teacher.

• Assist the school nurse during health screenings.

• Speak at career day.

• Speak to your child's class about your family's religion or ethnic traditions.

• Help out on author day.

• Man a booth at the school carnival or book fair.

interesting items for the science table or class estimation jar. There are also things you can do on the weekend or in the evening such as helping to clean the building or move tables or set up chairs for an event, helping plant flowers or put up playground equipment, or offering to babysit during parent-teacher conferences. Parents can also help by picking up items on teachers' or the school's wish list. For instance, many classrooms need things like plastic or paper bags, tissues, and old shirts for smocks.

I Want to Volunteer But My Child Doesn't Want Me To

For whatever reason, your child doesn't want you to volunteer in his classroom. (Maybe your child is worried you'll embarrass him, cramp his style, or spend the whole time talking about him with the teacher.) Okay. Now what?

You could, of course, tell your child, "Too bad. I'm coming whether or not you like it." There's nothing wrong with putting your foot down; you are in charge, after all. But you'd probably feel better if you felt welcomed so talk to your child. Find out what he is worried about. Offer to make a compromise or work around an issue. For example, you could agree not to use your last name so the students don't know "who you belong to." Or you could agree not to address or even look at your child while you're in the room. Chances are excellent your child's friends will welcome you so warmly that any fears you're going to embarrass him will quickly disappear. Another solution might be to come in on a trial basis. Ask your child to let you volunteer a few times before he decides how he feels.

If you've tried volunteering in your child's class and it just isn't working out or your child feels strongly from the get go, consider volunteering in another classroom. You can also do one of the many at-home or after-hours volunteer jobs listed above.

INSIDER TIP

Most teachers worship the ground volunteers walk on. There are a few, though, who don't welcome parents in the classroom. Your child's teacher doesn't have to appreciate your presence in your child's class. She should, however, allow you and other parents to come in. If your child's teacher repeatedly turns down your offer to come in and help and doesn't offer you a reasonable explanation, speak with the principal. (An acceptable explanation may include the class is testing that week or there's a student who is easily distracted by having another adult in the room.)

Sports, Spelling Bees, and All That Jazz (Band)

You're catching up with a friend, the mother of one of your daughter's classmates. "So, can you believe how expensive it is to rent an instrument?" she says.

"What are you talking about?" you ask.

"Band, of course! Your daughter is signed up, right?"

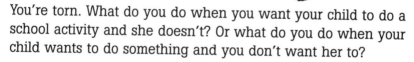

You used to play in the band. Those were some of the best times in your life and you've always expected your children to follow in your musical foot-steps. Of course you would have happily shelled out big bucks to rent an instru-ment . . . but your daughter never said a word about signups.

You're torn. What do you do when you want your child to do a school activity and she doesn't? Or what do you do when your child wants to do something and you don't want her to?

First, consider your motives. Ask yourself why it's so important to you that your child participates in a certain activity. Is it because you were in band, the State Spelling Bee champ, or played the lead in the spring musical and want to relive those things through your child? Or is your motivation your child's best interest? Do you really believe your child would benefit from, be successful at, or enjoy an activity? Maybe your child's enjoying the activity isn't the

143

problem. Maybe you're dragging your feet about allowing your child to sign up for something because it would take too much time or money. Are you worried about injury on the playing field? Or perhaps you're sure she'll dislike the activity or drop out. These are legitimate concerns. Being honest about your motivations will help you make the best decision for your child.

After you've examined your motives, consider your child's. Does she want to play soccer because her best friend does or because she has a real interest in soccer? Does your child want to be in the play but is nervous about auditioning? Is she worried about having enough time to do all the activities she wants? Ask her!

"I DIDN'T MAKE IT!"

Your child tried out for the play and didn't get the part she wanted. Worse yet, her best friend did! What's the best way to attend to a bruised ego?

Listen as your child vents. It hurts to fall short of your goals or not get something you feel you deserve. Let your child express her disappointment without immediately trying to cheer her up.

After comforting your child with a hug or two, help her gain some perspective. Choosing students to be in the play or on the math team is difficult. It's often a very subjective thing. There's also no way for you or your child to know how well other kids did at tryouts. Let your child know it's just someone else's turn to shine. Reassure your child that she will get a chance later.

Point out silver linings when they show up. Your child probably doesn't want to hear how it's a good thing she didn't get the part. But, if a better opportunity comes up down the road, be sure to mention it. ("Gee, it's a good thing you didn't get that part in the play or you wouldn't have been able to go take this cool art class!") Pointing out these things helps children see that things almost always work out for the best in the end.

Next, sit down with your child and address everyone's motivation and any other important issues. If, for example, your daughter is nervous about standing up in front of everyone at the spelling bee, you can offer to help her get over her fear. If she can't decide which instrument to play, arrange to take her to the music store to check out various instruments at her leisure. If you or your child is concerned about the time commitment of an activity, the two of you can agree to give it a try for a length of time before making a final decision.

If you must say no to your child for some reason, give them a simple, honest explanation and give them an alternative date. For example, "We have too many family commitments right now to take on play practice five days a week. You can try out for the spring musical."

Art Avalanche

Your child has brought home yet another backpack full of art. It's all brilliant, of course, rivaling any museum collection, but what are you going to do with it? You've already wallpapered the bathroom with old artwork, but you must put your foot down when it comes to doing the living room.

One way to stay ahead of an art avalanche is to face it head on. As soon as art comes home, determine its value. Sometimes, this task is easy because a piece is especially well done or you fall in love with it. But most of the time, appraising art is a challenge. Heaven forbid you accidentally throw out work your child wanted to save. To determine how meaningful a piece of art is to your child, ask questions. Often, just saying "Tell me more about this picture," will get a child talking. Listen to the story of how the piece came to be or how much time went into it. See if your child lights up when he talks about the piece. If your child shrugs and says something like, "Which picture? Oh, yeah, I did that last week," it's a pretty safe bet you can admire the picture briefly and toss it (when your child's asleep, of course) without repercussions. If you're not sure, consider having a "holding box" for art. This way, you can set aside work for a month or two. If your child doesn't ask about the piece, discreetly shove it to the bottom of the trash can with a clear conscience.

If you simply can't bear to throw out the art, there's still hope. Pictures can be recycled into wrapping paper or cut into one-of-a-kind stationery. Grandparents, aunts, uncles, cousins, and nursing home patients may be glad to have new artwork from up-and-coming artists. You can also cut a few squares from special pictures and use them to create a paper quilt or collage.

And remember. If all else fails—and you have the space—you can always save every shred of art your child brings home. Then when she leaves home, give it to her so she can wallpaper her house.

School Vacation and Transitions

The symptoms are unmistakable—restlessness, irritability, daydreaming, loss of motivation and concentration. And to top it off,

your kids are pretty squirrelly too. Yep. There's nothing like spring fever to bring discord to a household.

A highly contagious affliction that shuts down the brain as the outside temperature rises, spring fever happens in the best of families. Kids are hit the hardest as spring break looms on the calendar. And it's not just spring break you have to worry about. Looking forward to any break or going back to school after a long break (or even just a long weekend) can be challenging, causing such things as Holiday-itis or Summer Flu.

There is no known cure for any of these maladies, but rest assured parents can help:

Keep your family routine. Transitioning into summer or returning to school after a break is a trying time for families. Keeping your kids on schedule, as best you can, will help keep the family ship afloat. For example, as tempting as it is to let them stay up to play in the warmer evenings (or to send them to bed early because they are driving you nuts), insist your children maintain their bedtimes.

Reduce stress. With the excitement about the coming break or the anxiety over a test or end-of-the-year project that hasn't even been started, it's no wonder kids are wound tighter than a knot in a kite string. Make sure your kids are getting plenty of sleep and eating well. Physical activity such as an evening bike ride or a family game of kickball is a great way to reduce stress. Some kids may enjoy yoga or meditation or listening to music. Make sure your own kite string isn't wound too tightly, too. Enjoy some down time with your child—read a book, make cookies, or rent a movie and veg out in front of the TV together.

Dig down deep and find that extra bit of patience. Mother Nature has blessed humans with adrenaline in emergencies. Surely she's also given parents an extra dose of patience when it comes to dealing with wound-up or anxious kids. When things are really crazy around your house, dig deep and find the patience you need to count to ten (or a hundred). Remember what it was like to be a kid and know exactly how many days were left till summer break. Think about how hard it is to go back to work after a vacation and try to be more flexible and forgiving. And when your daughter is running around in her swimsuit and whining about wanting to drag the pool out when it's only 30 degrees, tell yourself, "That's not my child; it's just the 'fever' talking."

How to Keep Those Brain Cells Alive

What happens after a wonderful vacation when it's time for your child to go back to school? How can you avoid your child's brain turning into a sieve and everything she learned before she left school running right out? Whether you're staring at a long summer in front of you or just a two-week break between semesters, there's plenty of fun, easy, and often inexpensive ways to keep those brain cells alive.

Read! Read! Read! Join a book club or make going to the library a weekly affair. Visit a discount bookstore or search at garage sales.

Buy your child a journal and let her write. If your child is feeling ambitious, challenge her to write a play for the neighborhood kids to perform. For a short break, encourage your child to make a scrapbook of the family vacation.

Give your child a disposable camera and let him create a photo journal.

Start each day off with a new "word of the day." Have your child keep a tally of how many times she can use the word.

Challenge your child to memorize a list of all the states or the presidents. Or make a list of all the books he has read or words that rhyme with pickle.

Dump out the junk drawer and let your child organize items into categories. You can also dump all the toys you have in your house in the middle of the playroom and have your child sort the pile!

Let your child count the money in the change bucket.

Invest in some board games that require thinking and planning, or strategy games like chess or checkers. Challenge your child to put together a game tournament with the other kids in the neighborhood.

Visit museums or local historical sites.

Enroll your child at a summer sports, theater, or art camp.

Sign your child up for music lessons.

Encourage your child to start up his own business. There's a lot

to be learned by running your own "company" and even young kids can offer all kinds of services like pet sitting, pulling weeds, selling lemonade, picking up mail, shoveling sidewalks, helping to take down holiday decorations or ornaments, or reading to younger children.

Teacher Gifts

It's the end of the school year and you'd like to show your appreciation to the saint who taught your son to read and looked the other way when you let him go to school in slippers. Trouble is, you're not rolling in the green stuff. To top it off, you're as sick of giving the usual gifts as teachers are of getting them. What do teachers really want? Here's some unique and inexpensive ideas that don't include mugs, candles, soaps and lotions, or apples in any form:

Homemade goodies. Cookies, brownies, a loaf of bread, a gourmet lunch—anytime you don't have to cook and clean the dishes, food tastes extra delicious.

Tote bags. There's no such thing as having too many bags. Totes are handy things for teachers and simple to make using canvas bags and decorations found at any craft store.

Personalized stationery. There's plenty of great software that can help you do this. Better yet, have your child draw a design and take it to a print shop to make copies on colored paper. Add a few stamps and—ta da!—a way for your child's teacher to let everyone know the students have finally done her in and she's run off to Jamaica.

Letter of thanks. Why not use the first piece of that personalized stationery to write your child's teacher a letter of thanks? Have your child write one, too. Include a favorite memory from the year, and maybe a photo.

Refrigerator magnets. Create one-of-a-kind magnets by having your child draw a picture or write a favorite quote on a small index card. Cover the card with clear contact paper or laminating paper and add two strips of magnetic tape to the back.

Frames. Wondering what to do with all those puzzles with missing pieces? (Besides throwing them out, of course.) Paint the pieces and glue them collage-style onto an inexpensive wooden frame. Get out the glitter if you're feeling really adventurous.

Classroom apron. Buy a canvas tool apron at a hardware store and then use fabric paint and plastic jewels to jazz it up. It's great for holding all kinds of things (spare pencils, stickers, a rubber stress release ball to squeeze) when walking around the classroom.

Coffee spoons. OK, just one variation on the coffee mug theme. Dip the bottoms of plastic spoons into melted dark and white chocolate. Tie them up with ribbon and instructions to use the spoons for stirring coffee or hot chocolate.

Water bottle and lemon drops. Every fall, teachers are plagued by laryngitis. Help prevent this by presenting your child's teacher with a special or hand-decorated water bottle and candy to suck on.

Cards, wrapping paper, and gift bags. Who doesn't like having a stash of these items? Stock up on seasonal and all-occasion wrapping paper and cards when you find them on sale.

Gift certificates. This is the gift that teachers brag to other teachers about getting. Consider a gift card from a restaurant, spa, movie theater, bookstore, video store, or teacher supply store.

Adopt an animal. Either adopt an animal at the zoo or donate to her favorite cause.

Summer survival kit. Put together a gift bag filled with those things a teacher might need for summer: sunglasses, a paperback book, sunscreen, a button that says "I'm on recess," a map showing the way back to school.

The gift of time. Offer to come in after school lets out and help tear down the classroom.

Resources

GOING TO SCHOOL FOR THE FIRST TIME

Miss Bindergarten Gets Ready for Kindergarten by Joseph Slate, illustrated by Ashley Wolff (Puffin Books, 2001)

First Day Jitters by Julie Danneberg, illustrated by Judy Love (Charlesbridge Publishing, 2000)

Junie B. Jones and The Stupid Smelly Bus by Barbara Park, illustrated by Denise Brunkus (Random House Children's Books, 1992)

MAKING FRIENDS

How to Be a Friend: A Guide to Making Friends and Keeping Them by Laurie Krasny Brown and Marc Brown (Little, Brown, 2001)

Hey, New Kid! by Betsy Duffey, illustrated by Ellen Thompson (Puffin Books, 1998)

How Kids Make Friends: Secrets for Making Lots of Friends, No Matter How Shy You Are by Lonnie Michelle (Freedom Publishing Co., 1997)

NOT FITTING IN

Odd Velvet by Mary Whitcomb, illustrated by Tara Calahan King (Chronicle Books, 1998)

Stand Tall, Molly Lou Melon by Patty Lovell, illustrated by David Catrow (G.P. Putnam's Sons, 2001)

Helping the Child Who Doesn't Fit In by Stephen Nowick Jr. Ph.D., Marshall Duke Ph.D. (Peachtree Publishers, 1992)

FEARS AND ANXIETIES

Monsters Under the Bed and Other Childhood Fears: Helping Your Child Overcome Anxieties, Fears and Phobias by Stephen W. Garber, Ph.D. (Villard Books, 1993)

Helping Your Anxious Child by Ronald Rapee Ph.D., Susan Spence Ph.D., Vanessa Cobham, Ph.D., Ann Wignall, M. Psych. (New Harbinger Publications, 2000)

SCHOOL LUNCHES

Brown Bag Success: Making Healthy Lunches Your Kids Won't Trade by Sandra K. Nissenbery, MS.RD and Barbara N. Pearl MS.RD (Wiley, 1998)

The School Lunchbox Cookbook by Miriam Jacobs (Globe Pequot, 2003)

American School Food Service Association
700 South Washington St., Suite 300
Alexandria, VA 22314
703-739-3900, www.asfsa.org

BUS SAFETY

National Safety Council
www.nsc.org
1121 Spring Lake Drive
Itasca, IL 60143-3201
630-285-1121

National Highway Traffic
Safety Administration
www.nhtsa.gov
400 7th St. SW
Washington DC 20590

DISABILITIES/LEARNING DISABILITIES

Negotiating the Special Education Maze by Winifred Anderson, Stephen Chitwood, Deidre Hayden (Woodbine House, 1997)

Learning Disabilities
Association of America
www.ldanatl.org
4156 Liberty Road
Pittsburgh, PA 15234-1349
412-341-1515

Americans with Disabilities Act
www.usdoj.gov
800-514-0301 (voice)
800-514-0383 (TDD)

GIFTED CHILDREN

The Gifted Kids' Survival Guide for Ages 10 and Under by Judy Galbraith. M.A. (Free Spirit, 1998)

The Survival Guide for Parents of Gifted Kids: How to Understand, Live With, and Stick Up for Your Gifted Child by Sally Yahnke Walker, Ph.D. (Free Spirit, 2002)

Stand Up For Your Gifted Child: How to Make the Most of Kids' Strengths at School and at Home by Joan Franklin Smutny (Free Spirit, 2000)

BULLIES/TEASING

Bullies Are a Pain in the Brain and *Cliques* by Trevor Romain (Free Spirit Publishing, 1997)

Cliques, Phonies and Other Baloney by Trevor Romain (Free Spirit Publishing, 1998)

The Recess Queen by Alexis O'Neill, illustrated by Laura Huliska-Beith (Scholastic, 2002)

Easing the Teasing: Helping Your Child Cope with Name-Calling, Ridicule, and Verbal Bullying by Judy Freedman (McGraw-Hill/Contemporary Books, 2002)

The Bully, The Bullied, and the Bystander: From Preschool to High School—How Parents and Teachers Can Help Break the Cycle of Violence by Barbara Coloroso (HaperResource, 2004)

Mom, They're Teasing Me: Helping Your Child Solve Social Problems by Michael Thompson, Ph.D., Lawrence J. Cohen, Ph.D., with Catherine O'Niell Grace (Ballantine Books, 2002)

Web sites: www.stopbullyingnow.hrsa.gov

HOMEWORK

How to Do Homework Without Throwing Up by Trevor Romain (Free Spirit, 1997)

Bright Minds, Poor Grades: Understanding and Motivating Your Under-achieving Child by Michael D. Whitley, Ph.D. (Perigee Books, 2001)

Ending the Homework Hassles by John Rosemond (Andrew McMeel Publishing, 1990)

Web sites: www.infoplease.com/homework

OTHER HELPFUL RESOURCES

No More Misbehavin': 38 Difficult Behaviors and How to Stop Them by Michele Borba, Ed.D. (Jossey-Bass, 2003)

No Child Left Behind Act
www.ed.gov/nclb/landing.jhtml